STACK IT UP!

STACK IT UP!

Stop Losing Talent;
Build the Next Level Together

JANEEN M. LATINI

NEW YORK

NASHVILLE • MELBOURNE • VANCOUVER

Stack It Up!
Stop Losing Talent; Build the Next Level Together

Published in New York, New York, by Morgan James Publishing in partnership with Difference Press. Morgan James is a trademark of Morgan James, LLC.
www.MorganJamesPublishing.com

The Morgan James Speakers Group can bring authors to your live event. For more information or to book an event visit The Morgan James Speakers Group at www.TheMorganJamesSpeakersGroup.com.

ISBN 9781683504306 paperback
ISBN 9781683504313 eBook
ISBN 9781683504320 hardcover
Library of Congress Control Number: 2017901347

Cover Design by:
Chris Treccani
www.3dogdesign.net

Interior Design by:
Chris Treccani
www.3dogdesign.net

In an effort to support local communities, raise awareness and funds, Morgan James Publishing donates a percentage of all book sales for the life of each book to Habitat for Humanity Peninsula and Greater Williamsburg.

Get involved today! Visit
www.MorganJamesBuilds.com

DEDICATION

For the leaders who trust me,
For the staff who inspire me,
You are the reason this book exists.

TABLE OF CONTENTS

WHY I WROTE THIS BOOK

I've reached a point where I really do love my life. I love myself, I love my family, I love my career, and I flat out live in-love. This, I will admit, was not always the case. In fact, I had a lot of thoughts that seemed to indicate the opposite:

- I just have to get through this (fill in the blank).
- Everything will be so much better once X happens, or Y is completed.
- I wish it was different, but it's not, so I'm just going to have to live with it.
- Ugh, there's just not enough time...I don't have any more to give.
- I'm just going to step away for a little while and re-group ... sigh.

It's funny, because I didn't realize how not-in-love I was when I was saying those things. Those were my down times, periods when I felt spent, overwhelmed, or at best, neutral. However, I actually believed I sounded realistic, healthy, balanced, pragmatic, and the like. I really wanted to be all of those honorable words and more. I believe we all do, and even more importantly, I believe we have conditioned ourselves to expect that these down times are just an unavoidable part of life. Our experiences have taught us to "wait it out," or to "push through it," because "what goes down must come up."

But as Einstein so eloquently stated, insanity is "doing the same thing over and over again and expecting different results." Pushing through a down time with the same behavior patterns and thought processes will not make things better. It will simply make us feel tired and disappointed. Doing more of the same will not bear different results; it will give us the false sense that we have done everything we could, without any return.

I submit to you that these down times serve a purpose. The purpose is to not encourage us to work harder and longer, the way most of us currently do. The purpose is to wake us up, and encourage us to look at our world with different eyes.

If you looked in the mirror and didn't like your hair, what would you do? Would you shrug it off because it's just hair and it doesn't really matter? Would you tell a story that you used to have great hair when you had more free time/were younger/had a different stylist, ahh those were the days... Would you make a note that you need to do something about it before the next holiday/party/photo op? Or, would you call the best stylist you know and make an appointment to change it?

The magic happens in two parts. Part one is noticing that something needs to change because it is an indication that you have new awareness, new eyes. Part two arrives as the invitation to take new action, to choose to create change. When you choose to respond to that invitation, the magic of leadership happens. That is the magic of taking a stand and investing in making change.

No one aspires to mediocrity. No one aspires to live tired. No one desires to be frustrated. There is no medal of honor for living in these feeling states. There is no reward. The fact of the matter for me is that I was out of balance, out of gratitude, out of love, and therefore, disengaged without even knowing it! My negative thoughts had come to be my monologue, my cover story. I now know that when I hear those words, it's time to get to work – in a different way.

The truth is that this was not a one-off personal issue. I was (and am) in good company when it comes to leaders who have hit frustration. It was, and is, an epidemic affecting the workforce. Leagues of smart, experienced leaders have fallen out-of-love and out of sync with themselves and their organizations. They want everything and everyone to be successful, but instead are experiencing drops in productivity, hiccups in client delivery, and an exodus of staff, including the ones no one thought would ever leave.

And so, as leaders, what do we find ourselves talking about: the market is down, the attrition is up, the fun factor has waned, and our staff aren't engaged. What happened to the hard-core professionals we used to have? And then we wonder, why is this so hard to fix? What are we missing? We re-examine salaries, we measure benefits, we increase "opportunities," and we open calendars to generate more "access." We spend time talking and thinking about the things that don't seem to be working anymore. We listen to learn what our employees want, but feel they aren't getting. We consult the human capital experts and ask them to review the critical factors affecting employee engagement and retention. Yet the numbers remain unchanged.

This book is for those leaders. The leaders who care, who see there is an issue, and who have been struggling to put the happy back into their teams and to retain their top talent. This is for you, leader, the one who knows it will be so much better when the bleeding stops, the staffing stabilizes, the retention rate rises, and the business grows. You are correct. It WILL be better then. "Then", however, starts now. "Better" starts now.

"Wisdom means to choose now what will make sense later. I am learning every day to allow the space between where I am and where I want to be, to inspire me and not terrify me."

TRACEE ELLIS ROSS

CHAPTER 1:

Introduction

To the CEOs of small and mid-size businesses: this one is for you. To the mid-level managers in large corporations who are running small or mid-size businesses within a larger organization: this one is for you. To the leaders with a vision of an amazing business, offering top quality service with the smartest, most dedicated staff in existence: this one is for you. To the leaders who have chosen to manage a business and lead people to success in doing so: this, my friends, is for you.

I am calling all of you CEOs. In your role leading the team, you are the CEO. Own that role. Own that you are the leader. Own that you are the "top" in your organization, whether you are part of a larger ecosystem or not—in this role, you are the top. Your vision charts the course and who you are matters. You must embody the role of leader and not leave it to anyone else. It's you. So let's do this!

Dear CEO, you're amazing. I admire you in a way you might not know. You had a dream, a passion, a desire to serve, and you went for it! I know you also wanted to make money and build a sustainable business, but that was most likely so that you could afford to do what you wanted to do, to do what you love, to serve the customers/clients you knew you could help. There was a problem you knew how to solve, and so you solved it!

I bet it was also scary sometimes. Scary in the same way holding your breath and jumping off the high diving board into the deep end of the pool was scary. How cold is the water going to be? Will I float to the top before running out of air? What if water goes up my nose? Who is waiting and watching poolside, ready to cheer me on? Am I a good enough swimmer to even attempt this? The fact is, your desire to jump in outweighed any possible answers to all of those questions, and they became irrelevant. It had to happen that way, or you wouldn't have jumped. In that moment, fear transformed into courage. You took the reservoir of nervous energy and channeled it straight into excitement and courage. You jumped! That same exact process of converting anxiety into excitement and activating it forward is what you did when you started your business. So, whether you brew craft beer, stitch your own designer clothing, imagine creative kids' parties, design indoor spaces to fit people's lifestyles, support others' financial planning, code innovative software, develop apps, or coach and consult with others to help them live their best lives—you are putting yourself and your love into the world all day, every day. You are giving, being, and doing all that you can to be of service to others.

That is nothing short of amazing.

It took a lot to stand up your business. You devoted your time, your money, and your heart to it. You probably gave up countless hours of sleep and made sacrifices that nobody knows about but you. I bet some of them included the scariest propositions of your life, laden with risk and potential financial burden. Not to mention the thousands of questions you received from well-meaning folks who were worried about whether you'd really thought this through, if you were sure about it, if you'd thought about health insurance, "paid" time off, or some other pragmatic concern. At some point, you made the decision that this business would happen and it was going to be successful, because quite frankly it needed to be, and the world would be lacking without it. Almost like magic, that is when your business blossomed. Things fell into place, the phone rang with potential clients, your inbox filled up, ideas became reality, and just like that, you were an entrepreneur, a business owner, a CEO.

The more you talked about the incredible product or service you were offering, the more people inquired about it. Soon, you were serving at a rapid pace and needed help to continue to serve and grow. Maybe you took to the Internet and used a service like Fiverr or Guru to acquire quick expert help on a specific issue. Maybe you thought "who are my smartest, most talented friends", and then asked them if they'd be interested in a side gig working with you on your passion project. Maybe you realized you needed consistent support and hired an assistant. Maybe you chose to outsource critical tasks by contracting with a brand specialist to professionalize your image or with a webmaster to mature your on-line presence. Maybe you added a few 1099s to serve specific clients or execute pieces of projects for you. Eventually, you took a deep breath and hired part-time staff–or even full-time staff. Go ahead, exhale. I know just remembering that transition made your heart race a little. That super-exciting time came wrapped in a blanket of anxiety. Totally normal, and you survived!

Whatever the path was, your business grew. It was no longer a "party of one" making things happen. In order to scale, you had to invest, which meant adding talented people to your business. You transcended the role of amazing individual contributor to become a manager/director/leader. You transitioned from running a business, to leading an organization of people. Did you get that? Running a business is one thing that you do;

leading an organization of human beings is another. Sure, they intersect and overlap but they are not one and the same.

Running a Business	Leading People
Building a Vision	Sharing a Vision
Business Strategy	People Strategy
Technical Skills	Management Skills
Task Execution	Task Integration
Listening to End Customers	Listening to Employees First
Making the Payroll	Rewarding Your Team
Zealot	Diplomat

The aspects of your personality that drove you to stand up your business are not the same ones that will make you an effective team leader. They are undeniably your strengths and they are what urged you to claim your space in the world as an entrepreneur, but the skills that will transform you into a successful CEO and leader of others are different. "Because you own the company, you're the boss," says business and leadership consultant and author Simon Sinek. "But you're not a leader until you make it your job to look after others."

This change from solopreneur to business leader is far more than task execution or payment for service. This change is the conscious choice to share your life's work, your passion, and your mission with another person, and trust them to love it (almost) as much as you do. While doing that, you also committed to their well-being: intellectually through meaningful work, financially through steady income, and socially/emotionally by offering a healthy business environment. Many people depict small and mid-size businesses as families. There is a reason for that, and it has nothing to do with size. It is about human dynamics, and yes, love. You see, in small businesses, everyone is inter-connected, much like a family. And in a small business there is no room for a rat race or an "every man for himself" mentality. The small business creed: all for one, one for all; we are all in this together. Large corporations like to see themselves that way, and often invest in team building within smaller business units or divisions to create a family of families, an extended family, so to speak.

Let's take a few minutes to review that critical transition when your vision, your business, transcended you and became an organization, a team effort. Whether your business became a team last week or five years ago doesn't matter. What matters is your experience of that transition, and the experience of those who joined you on the journey.

REFLECTION POINT:
Inviting Someone to Your Party

✓ Who was the first person you added to your business?

_____

_____

_____

✓ How did you recruit him/her?

_____

_____

_____

✓ What offer did you make? What did you promise?

_____

_____

_____

✓ How did you portray the opportunity?

_____

_____

_____

✓ When you asked him/her why he/she wanted to join
  your business, why now, what was his/her answer?
  (His/her interest, his/her perception of you.)

_____

_____

_____

✓ What did you do to welcome that person into your
  company? (On-boarding, transition in.)

_____

_____

_____

✓ If you had the opportunity revisit this moment, would
  you? What would you do differently or what advice
  might you offer yourself? What would you give yourself
  a high-five for?

_____

_____

_____

Spend a moment here. This first hiring, extending your first invitation
to another person to join your team demonstrates your courageousness.
If you remember this event as a time of great vulnerability, that is even
more evidence of your courage. Adding talent to your team added

strength and capacity. It also added responsibility and created a new role for you as the leader. The same action that offers streamlining in one area brought complexity in another. Now that you have a team, you probably want to keep it!

Retention and Attrition: Why These Metrics Matter

If the departure of staff didn't affect you, you wouldn't be reading this book. The truth is, to maintain organizational health you must retain top talent. Similarly, to maintain organizational health, you must experience attrition. In any organization, moderate turnover is necessary. Just as a gardener prunes the garden, you need at times to cut back your organization so that it can grow. Attrition is required for an organization to maintain its health. Too little attrition results in stagnation. Too much attrition results in gaps in service, knowledge, and, potentially, an inability to deliver products. The job of the CEO is to manage the organization and its footprint to not only keep pace with business but to plan for growth. According to 2015 research, these tasks remain challenging and are positioned at the top of the priority list.

- 40% of companies are reporting loss of personnel as a top concern (Society for Human Resource Management, or SHRM)
- The top three challenges faced by HR organizations today are turnover, employee engagement, and succession planning (SHRM)
- 49% of HR leaders named retention and leadership development programs as the top priority among talent management goals (Saba Software)

So, what about the numbers? How can we use the retention/attrition metrics that are so closely tracked and so often discussed to indicate health? Before providing general guidelines in regard to these numbers, it is imperative to offer caution that these numbers must be considered within the context of the organizational environment and life-stage. An organization embarking on great change such as acquisition of another company or launch of a new product or service should expect to see different numbers than an organization that is in a fairly steady state, maintaining production and organizational structure. Metrics are useful because they offer us a lens through which to tell a story. When an organization sees attrition numbers spike, it is an indicator of change. People are opting out of the organization. This could indicate trauma, or this could indicate growth. Getting behind the numbers to understand what is happening and why is the real value of monitoring the metrics.

Let's review some basic threshold numbers. The steady-state quantitative indicator of "healthy" attrition typically lands in the 10-15% range. If your organization has attrition hovering around 10-15%, and therefore retention securely in the 85-90% range, by the numbers, your organization is in good health and above average.

Many factors play into the attrition numbers, and should be expected. For example, recruiting is an imperfect science, and some hires are mis-hires. Up to 10% of all recruiting is an unpreventable mismatch. Selection takes place bi-directionally, an individual choosing the organization and the organization choosing the individual. It is not uncommon for the match process to be imprecise. Organizations grow and change, as do people. Even with the rise in telework options, sometimes physical moves and family changes cause someone to resign from one job and seek another. It is not unusual for people to make an employment change for reasons having nothing to do with "lack" or "problems" at their current job. The metrics on average length of employment at a specific company have radically changed over the last two decades. We no longer see employees staying with an employer for the majority of their career. According to the Bureau of Labor Statistics, the average worker currently holds ten different jobs before age 40, and this number is projected to grow. Forrester Research predicts that today's youngest workers will hold 12 to 15 jobs in their lifetime.

2016 statistics available on this topic include:

- 74% of all workers are satisfied with their jobs; 66% of those are still open to new employment (Jobvite)
- One in three workers will change jobs in the next six months (Saba Software)
- 42% of millennials expect to change jobs at least every one to three years (Jobvite)
- 44% of millennials say, if given the choice, they expect to leave their current employers in the next two years (Deloitte)
- 66% of millennials say, if given the choice, they expect to leave their current employers by 2020 (Deloitte)
- 49% of Americans plan to spend six years or more at their current company (Finn Futures)

In regard to newly hired staff, the old adage rings true: you never have a second chance at a first impression. With new team members, the first six to twelve months are critical. Even more pointedly, the first day and week offer powerful opportunities to welcome and build a relationship. The initial interactions with a manager, with being given a work assignment, with meeting a client/customer, and with receiving feedback, are all critical moments that serve as decision points for that employee when determining if this job is the right one and if this organization is truly the best match. If those initial experiences are positive, and when taking stock of the first year, he/she has a generally positive highlight reel, it is likely that employee will stay with your organization for two years or more. If you reach two and a half years with an employee, and both you (employer/manager) and the employee are happy, you will likely enjoy that person as a member of your team for at least five years.

- 33% of employees knew whether they would stay at their company long-term after being on the job for one week or less; 63% had decided within the first month (Ultimate Software).

At five years, another hurdle presents itself. People tend to make five-year plans, and are taught to look at their careers in windows of two, five, and ten years. Have you seen an exit of staff around the five-year mark? Are you hearing that some of your well-trained, four- to six-year staff are feeling antsy? This is not a surprise. If there is not a clear next step, a path to promotion both in title and earning capacity, they will start looking for other options. High performers don't want status quo; these people are on the move!

What does this mean, practically speaking? If you are going to make the investment to hire someone into your business (and it is an investment—it costs money to hire), then you really must invest in them. Replacing staff at all tenures is an expensive proposition:

- $11 billion is lost annually due to employee turnover (Bloomberg BNA)
- Each year, the average company loses 20-50% of its employee base (Bain & Company)
- 33% of workers who have been with a company less than three years are engaged, compared with 29% of those who have been with a company three to nine years and 30% of those who have been with a company for over ten years (Gallup)
- Cost of replacing entry level employees: 30-50% of their annual salary (ERE Media)

- Cost of replacing mid-level employees: 150% of their annual salary (ERE Media)
- Cost of replacing high-level or highly specialized employees: 400% of their annual salary (ERE Media)

Consider this: Your employees are your first customers. They are the first people you made an offer to, and the first ones to have your commitment. Therefore, your first job is to serve them. This is the basic premise and key to operationalizing retention, so I want to plant this seed right now. If your view of employees is that they exist to help YOU, it is time to take a pause and consider your framing. Would you want to spend all day, every day, with someone who viewed you as there only to serve them, to respond to requests, and to say yes ma'am or yes sir? No, you wouldn't. That's likely one of the reasons why you started your own business, whether you know it or not. So take a moment and think about this: what is your frame of mind when collaborating with your employees?

"The way your employees feel is the way your customers will feel. And if your employees don't feel valued, neither will your customers."
SYBIL F. STERSHIC

The customer is always right. Sound advice that was made popular by entrepreneur pioneers like Henry Ford and Marshall Field. You hear it today in every industry, and it is the motto of all customer service providers. I absolutely understand and agree with this sentiment. As the leader of an organization of people, your first customer is your employee. They have chosen to work with and for you. They have made a choice to enter into a contract or agreement to serve your customers in exchange for you serving them. Your service is not just pay and benefits. Your service is sharing your time and talent with them, and investing in their future as well. You have built an ecosystem. The health of one affects the health of all. Serve your employees and they will in turn serve your customers.

- Customer retention rates are 18% higher on average when employees are highly engaged (Cvent)

> *"Always treat your employees exactly as you want them*
> *to treat your best customers."*
> **STEPHEN R. COVEY**

REFLECTION POINT:
Interacting with Team Members

✓ Think about the last conversation you had with a team member. Got it? Ok, keep reading.

_____

_____

_____

✓ What was your purpose for that conversation?

_____

_____

_____

✓ What was in your mind when you started the dialogue?

_____

_____

_____

✓ What was in your heart when you started the dialogue?

_____

_____

_____

✓ How did it go for you?

_____

_____

_____

✓ What happened?

_____

_____

_____

✓ How did you feel at the end?

_____

_____

_____

✓ What did your team member say or do to indicate how the exchange went for them?

_____

_____

_____

✓ Could this have gone differently?

_____

_____

_____

Was this interaction a good example of a typical interaction with team members? If yes, great. You have a good baseline of how you approach your team. What was in your mind and heart when you started the conversation provides us with information about your frame of thought regarding the team member and the interaction. This is also an indicator of if and how you set intention.

Effective conversations (one-to-one or in a group setting) happen when an intention is set for them. Setting the intention allows our brains and hearts to align with the direction we selected. When you set an intention, the words you choose, how you deliver them, your energy, and your presence are all affected. Everything about you is aligned and on board to support your message delivery or interaction. All of this determines the quality of the interaction.

I devote a section of *Love to Lead. Lead to Love.* to the power of intention if you want to explore it more. It truly is a cornerstone for our interactions with others.

If the interaction you thought about before was not representative of your typical interactions with team members, select one that is and run through the questions again. This is an important review to get a sense of your typical approach. If each interaction with a team member bears little resemblance to those with other team members, it would be worth your time to take stock of the quality and nature of each of these relationships. It will also be helpful to you to reflect upon how you view yourself and what role you play in the organization.

When the Numbers Become a Warning Flag

If your attrition number has surpassed 20% and/or has been climbing, it is time to take a look at what is going on. This is a sign that what is happening inside your organization is only working 80% of the time. 80% isn't a bad number, but it is a definite warning sign. If your customer satisfaction was at 80%, would you be satisfied? I'm going to submit that you would not. How do I know this? You probably wouldn't even place a bid on an eBay item if the seller had only a satisfaction rate of only 80%. You would continue to shop around for someone in the high 90s, preferably at 100% positive.

You know that customer satisfaction is the name of the game, and I'm pretty sure since you are devoted to service that you want your customers to be happy. This is a basic tenet of business. Good business and happy customers bring more business. If your employee retention rate is at 80%, that means that your customer satisfaction rating, as a leader, is at 80%. Your first customers are your team members, and they vote with their feet. How does it feel to be at 80%? Whether we like it or not – that number bears power.

This may be a little baffling, especially if your end customer satisfaction is in the high 90s. What that means is that you are over-performing–and likely other members of your team are over-performing–to keep the trains running and to not let your customers feel the impact. This is how you get through the crisis, but this is not a sustainable operation. If your end customer satisfaction rate is even lower than 80%, you're feeling the heat and so is your team. More than one scenario could be at play here. Either the over-performing of a fractured team has gone on too long and the cracks are showing, or there is under-performing happening. In the face of stress, fight or flight kicks in, and in the workplace that results in over- or under-performing. Neither is sustainable.

> *"To win in the marketplace you must first win in the workplace."*
> **DOUG CONANT**

What's the business impact of 80% retention and 20% attrition? Cost and investment. You are now bearing the cost of investing in replacement recruiting, transition plans, and possibly the re-distribution of work, especially if there is a gap in time between when employee

X leaves and employee Y replaces them. There is the financial cost of recruiting, and the energy cost to you and to the rest of your team. Also note that there is a tax being levied on the retained employees. They are picking up the slack, wondering what's happening, and with each departure, they are re-evaluating the status of their employment. You are also now experiencing the cost of managing the changing dynamic of your team. In a small business, if two of ten employees leave, that shift is felt.

Workload and processes are impacted certainly, but so are emotions. If two of your ten family members disappear, would it impact you? What would happen to the dialogue within your family? By the way, the majority of this will not be spoken about to you. Whatever you are hearing in regard to these concerns or musings is evidence of the high-trust relationships you have developed with certain members of your team. Or, it is evidence of what they are comfortable sharing with you. Therefore, be advised that there is at least three times more of this dialogue going on that you will never hear about, ever. Unless, you ask...

If you do talk with your employees and are consistent about remaining open to discussion and are timely in your responses to their suggestions or requests, you are likely to receive more honest feedback when you inquire about this topic. You will never receive all of the feedback, and you don't need it. Once you have a few solid examples and themed responses, you can begin responding and implementing changes to address the most pressing needs. Waiting for more data is simply an excuse to delay action. I know it doesn't feel that way. It feels like you want to be as informed as possible so you can make the best choices, but in reality standing still and waiting for data is false forward progress. You are deferring the leadership move–and there is nobody else to make it.

One other aspect I would be remiss to not mention is, where is the attrition coming from? Are you losing people from the same job function or from the same sub-team? Or is it distributed across the business?

For example, you may notice that you have had turnover in your communications division. Maybe the first person who left was a designer who found a new gig that offered him role enhancement (to manage a team of designers). Then maybe you lost a marketing content author who cited a need for diversity in her work. Then maybe you received a resignation from a client relationship manager, who didn't really offer a reason but allowed you to believe it was due to family obligations.

Each of these could have been totally independent and for the stated reasons above. However, the departure of three team members within the same functional group would lead me to investigate the operations of that division. This is not an indictment of that division manager or of you. This is simply the flag to spend some time looking and listening to what is happening with that group. If your attrition is sprinkled across your business, this is an indication that something systemic is happening. Something about how the business is managed is not acceptable to the staff, and they are choosing to leave. Have your business processes changed? Has your business grown? Are your service offerings different? Have the service level agreements or expectations of staff evolved? How about you? Are you a different leader than you were last year?

It is inevitable that something has changed in your business. For businesses to sustain, they must grow and adapt. Nothing is static. The question is, are your changes in support of your mission and in support of your staff and customers? Or have business decisions been made without regard to the people impact? Sometimes the CEO in us who is used to being the CEO, CFO, CIO, CTO–all rolled into one–forgets the CHCO (Chief Human Capital Officer) role that is so critical to play as a business grows. Business decisions ALL impact the people in an organization. Underestimating the people impact of business decisions is the Achilles heel of leaders and the most common mistake made.

REFLECTION POINT:

Who Is Still at Your Party?

✓ Is employee #1 still with you? How about employee
  #2? Maybe employee #3?

  _____

  _____

  _____

✓ If so, what is different today than when they started?
  What is the same?

  _____

  _____

  _____

✓ Are they doing the same roles as when you hired
  them? Have they taken on new roles?

  _____

  _____

  _____

✓ Do you spend the same amount of time with them
  as you originally did? What are the states of your
  relationships?

  _____

  _____

  _____

✓ Have you asked them what makes them stay?

  _____

  _____

  _____

✓ If one or more employees did not stay, what were the circumstances of the departures?

_____

_____

_____

✓ What were their stated reasons for leaving?

_____

_____

_____

✓ Where did they go?

_____

_____

_____

✓ Were these career changes, life changes, or job changes?

_____

_____

_____

✓ How did you feel about the departures?

_____

_____

_____

✓ Did you remain in touch?

_____

_____

_____

It is important to review who has stayed and who has left, and your relationships with them. There is something to learn from each of these people. And, for those who have left, you never know when you may want to invite them back.

CHAPTER 2:

Goodbye Is Never Easy

Sometimes staff choose to leave and it hurts. Sometimes staff leave and it is a relief. Sometimes it is both. Sometimes it is neither. All of these scenarios are worth delving into, because they hold the key to where you are in managing your organization. This information, you will see, is critical to your overall business health and success.

We have all lost staff. We have all had to accept a resignation letter. We have all had to deliver a termination. I have never met a leader who enjoyed any of the various scenarios of staff departure. Even the times when a leader must terminate someone for unethical behavior, or something of an equivalently grievous nature, there is no joy or satisfaction in that. That type of termination just stirs up doubts about the hiring process, your ability to judge character (the how-did-I-not-see this-earlier quandary), or the performance-monitoring system.

Whenever something goes wrong, leaders look for answers. Invested, tuned-in leaders look inward. What was it about me that allowed this to happen? You see, that is the leadership component of it, seeking your own culpability. Being the leader means you have a role in everything that happens, explicitly, implicitly, or comp licitly. And let's be honest, none of us ever want to see something not work out. Looking inward is a powerful self-examination of one's role in the situation. It allows you to reflect your leadership stance and assess if it serves your organization as best as it can. It is, however, not sufficient on its own. There are external factors that must be examined as well when assessing organizational health. Chapter 5 is devoted to those.

Healthy Goodbyes – Positive Voluntary Attrition

There are two types of positive voluntary attrition discussed in this book: 1) the offer you would be crazy to refuse, and 2) the life-is-short choice. Both of these scenarios are bittersweet. In both scenarios, a high-performing, valued team member chooses to leave your business for all the right reasons, and you are genuinely happy for her and supportive of her new adventure. Believe it or not, this reflects well on you and your business. Of course, you don't like the fact that she is leaving the team. That part is not enjoyable, so there is no need to pretend that it is. It's a loss. The fact that it is a loss means that you had a valued, healthy working relationship. You don't miss someone you struggled to relate to; you don't miss someone who underperformed; you miss the people who made work easy and fun, and who consistently contributed to the business.

The offer you would be crazy to refuse

We have all been there. One of your star performers asks for a private meeting. Naturally, you schedule the meeting immediately. Only when she starts to talk, you know this conversation is going somewhere you had not planned for. You aren't shocked, but you are a little caught off-guard and, as previously mentioned, a bit bummed. Your superstar has been recognized as a superstar by the outside world. At a recent trade show, she made a fabulous impression on competitors and clients. You watched as she deftly answered questions, generated referrals and demoed the new product line with ease. She was a natural relationship-builder, completely comfortable talking with others. One of the potential clients (think big, blue chip big) took notice of this and thought she would be the perfect fit for their company's open client relationship manager requisition. Sometime after the trade show, that firm reached out to her for an informational interview. She wasn't looking for a job, but a huge opportunity found her. She knows she wouldn't have this offer had it not been for your support and encouragement, and she is grateful for all you have done to grow her skills and career. She wants to make sure the transition is smooth and so she offers three weeks' notice.

Congratulations–this kind of departure is a sign that you are doing it right! You identified a highly talented person and supported her development. She became even more attractive to other employers, and hence received an offer to try something at the next level. Her work with you not only grew her skills and reputation, it grew her self-esteem, and encouraged her to dream even bigger. The fact that her bigger dreams didn't include your company is not a slight; it is a compliment. You played a role in putting even more goodness and quality out into the world, and the qualities you instilled will travel with her as she continues to serve clients and customers elsewhere. I understand it may not feel this way at first. For the good of all, give this thought some consideration.

Succession planning exists for exactly that purpose. How can you be continuously growing your next level leaders within your organization while also having a healthy pipeline of potential recruits? There is an entire specialty designed to help you do this. If all of your high-performers stayed in place forever, 1) they wouldn't remain high-performing, and 2) there would be no succession and no upward mobility for the rest of your team.

Almost all organizations claim to have upward mobility and opportunity for anyone willing to take it. As the leader, it is your responsibility to determine if that is true or merely illusory. If you notice a trend of high-performers choosing to take their career to the next level at a different organization, this is a sign that the opportunities for growth you believe are available, may not be.

- 74% of all workers are satisfied with their jobs; 66% of those are still open to new employment (Jobvite)
- 37% of employees have searched for jobs while at their current job (Jobvite)

The life-is-short choice

The second type of positive voluntary attrition is when someone leaves your organization for a truly personal reason, for example: relocating to another part of the country for family reasons, changing their lifestyle, or choosing to leave the industry you are in and try something completely different. This is when an exit cannot be prevented and, frankly, shouldn't be. These exits should be met with grace and gratitude for the time and service provided and with support for the next adventure.

Chris was a highly successful manager in his company. He started as an individual contributor and became quickly known as a high-performer and a fast learner. He helped Sarah, one of the senior managers, develop a new product and sell it to their customer base. Customers loved it and sales picked up. Sarah and the management team selected Chris to be one of the product managers for the new offering and Chris built a team to support the work and clients. He was one of three managers selling the new product, and his sales were consistently the highest. Chris received regular recognition, annual pay raises, and was even given more flexibility with his hours and work location. This was very appealing to him! He had extra time at the batting cages to coach his baseball team.

Good work earned more good work and good rewards. Chris was happy, Sarah was happy, and the team was happy.

One day, Chris requested a meeting with Sarah, who thought nothing of it since they work together so closely. This meeting, however, was something different. Chris shared with Sarah that he planned to resign. Sarah was a little surprised by this but not shocked. Sarah knew that Chris, while a successful product manager, had a deep athletic passion, especially for baseball. Chris shared with Sarah that he was opening a baseball academy. Everything he had learned about launching a new product line inspired him to take the leap and launch his own product, an innovative new concept for individual and team baseball coaching. Chris chose to make a career change and move into a wholly different business! Yet, he felt totally prepared because he could combine his business acumen with his athletic passion to make his living doing what he loved. Sarah responded with a huge smile and a hearty "Congratulations!"

Sarah didn't want to see Chris leave. He was her highest performer and likely the next to promote to senior manager. He was a trusted, valued, rewarded member of the team. He also had his own dream. Sarah truly experienced joy for Chris and shared in his excitement. This attrition showed evidence of Sarah's strong leadership. She developed Chris's talent, confidence, and trust. Chris shared openly with Sarah his hopes and plans. This relationship survived long beyond the job change. In fact, Sarah attended Chris's grand opening, and later his expansion party for off-season training camps and travel team excursions!

Healthy Goodbyes – Positive Involuntary Attrition

Involuntary attrition is when we have to terminate an employee. While I know typical retention discussions don't usually include involuntary attrition, I am including it here because of its leadership relevance. Leaders must at times make the decision to remove staff members from their teams. This is never easy, even though it is necessary. There are times when staff become toxic to the environment. I stated earlier that you are responsible for an ecosystem. In order to care for that ecosystem, you must ensure that there are not toxins polluting the environment.

Pollution comes in many forms within an organization. There are performance toxins, skill toxins, attitude toxins, and energy toxins, to name a few. I bet you have run into all of these and more. As the leader, your job is to maintain the environment and keep it free from pollution. Let's take a look at one of the most dangerous toxins to organizations, the type that appears to be a rose in the garden, not a predatory weed.

Doug

We all know this employee, I'll refer to him as Doug. Doug is the employee who makes you crazy. He is brilliant, truly. You hired him because he had uncommon ability. Something about his work was special, a cut above. You actually felt lucky when you found him. YES, this person will be fantastic on the team! I can't wait to see what we build together! And for a while, he was a shining star. Your customers loved him and the product quality was phenomenal. You would receive unsolicited feedback about how fabulous Doug's work was and how grateful people were for his products. He would, from time to time, go off the grid and you wouldn't hear from him for a couple of days. When he would re-surface there was a reasonable explanation and so you let it go. You told yourself and him, "as long as the work gets done and the clients are happy, it's fine."

Only it wasn't fine. The behavior troubled you. It was out of alignment with your values, and with the organizational values you established. It had a negative effect on you. You spent (wasted) time concerned about the cause, his well-being, the impacts, and thinking (unproductively) about how to handle it. This means you were distracted. Your energy and attention was pulled from the overall business, the team, and the clients.

This likely continued for a while. Doug's high performance, then absence, high performance, then mediocre performance, then absence, then last-minute save was a pattern that eventually gave way to confrontation. You revisited the expectations, and he promised to meet them. Maybe he asked for more flexibility, or a change in hours, or more autonomy, or something else that seemed reasonable, as long as the work was completed, on time, within budget, and of the highest quality. So, you made changes in the work agreement, and hoped everything would be fine. The rose blossomed again—this time bigger and brighter and fuller than before.

You started to relax. Your rosebush was blooming again. But when you looked up at the full garden, you found that while you were focused on just one plant some weeds cropped up. A family of rabbits decided to snack on your lettuce and a deer ate the heads off the tulips. The hidden cost of tending to Doug, your prize rosebush, was no longer hidden. To the store you went to buy some pesticide and fencing, with the hope that you could make repairs before the next client visit.

Back to business as usual, you regained your footing. Everything was humming along. The garden was growing. Some time passed and you actually believed the issue was resolved. Then, radio silence from Doug. The blush was off the rose, and the thorns were thick. This time it wasn't just you who noticed. Other employees were concerned, and client requests went unanswered. Now you really had a problem.

Since failure is never an option, the immediate production issue was resolved and client needs were met thanks to over-delivery on your part and the part of several other team members. It became painfully evident that this highly talented, bordering on genius employee was poisonous to your business. Although his work quality was second to none, his inconsistency and erratic behavior disrupted the flow of business. Other team members experienced unnecessary stress, and client managers were forced into cover stories. You found yourself searching for replacements and back-ups and caught yourself trying to modify your business processes to accommodate one employee sacrificing many for one.

That sentence hurt to read, didn't it? You never wanted to view that employee as problematic or poisonous to your business. He was brilliant and talented and you loved him. You invested in your business by hiring him, you invested in him by offering flexibility, and you also felt he was a friend. Yet there you were, left with the unfortunate and inevitable decision to part ways. You may have taken a few days, you may have taken a few weeks, you may have even carried around his termination letter in your folio for months. You held out hope that this would get better, that he would get back on board, that somehow the magic would return.

But when your decision was made, he made it for you. He made choices that were out of alignment with your personal values and your corporate values. No amount of talent could outweigh the value deficit. Once you delivered the news, you realized that you had not been breathing. Suddenly, there was air in your lungs, and you could hear your voice again. This is what relief feels like. You didn't realize how much pain you were in or your organization was in. The beautiful and thorny rosebush had morphed into a weed, strangling and starving the other plants in your garden.

Unhealthy Goodbyes – Negative Voluntary Attrition

Voluntary attrition has spiked in the last few years across industries. Some industries are feeling it worse than others, with Hospitality, Banking and Finance, and Healthcare leading the way (Compensation Force). That in no way means other industries are immune. The professional services and management consulting industries have had their fair share of voluntary attrition to contend with. There are many individual cases, but a review of commercially available data supports the empirical evidence I found during independent interviews.

The reason for voluntary attrition is never primarily financial. This sounds blasphemous. We always hear about people feeling overworked and underpaid, so how can it be that money is not one of the leading reasons? Take a look at the sentence one more time–overworked and underpaid. Money comes second of two factors there. The financial impact is typically the "insult" to the "injury." The vast majority of employees that voluntarily leave their employer leave because they no longer have a positive work experience. The critical aspects of the employee experience are detailed in a later chapter, and include career path, professional growth, organizational culture, and recognition. Pair a negative experience in any of those areas with a perceived financial inequity, and you have created the perfect environment for an attrition spike.

- The main factor in workplace discontent is not wages, benefits, or hours, but the boss (Gallup)
- 28% of employees would rather have a better boss than a $5,000 raise (Randstad)
- 36% of employees would give up $5,000 a year in salary to be happier at work (Randstad)
- 35% of employees say their top motivations for changing jobs are the desire for work/life balance and higher compensation; 25% say it's different work culture and wanting more challenging assignments (Right Management)
- 44% of employees say they would consider taking a job with a different company for a raise of 20% or less (Gallup)
- Just 37% of engaged employees would consider leaving for a 20% raise or less, compared to 54% of actively disengaged employees (Gallup)

Andrea

Here is an excerpt from my interview with Andrea, a healthcare professional:

My boss, Rae, was the kind of person that if she was happy, the whole world was happy. Otherwise, it was walking on eggshells working with her.

When I was trying to get pregnant, she was super supportive. I was older, and fertility is a sensitive topic. She had also been trying to have a baby. When I got pregnant, she was also supportive. Then I went out on maternity leave, and she barely kept in touch. Literally, she didn't call me for three months. I would reach out and get one-word replies. Even when I messaged her about my return to work, I got a simple "OK."

I returned from maternity leave. I saw Rae in the hallway on the way in. She didn't say anything to me, just kept working, so I waved and walked over to my office. I opened my office door. It was empty. Everything was gone. Desk, chairs, files, literally everything was gone. I didn't know what to do, I felt sick to my stomach. So I went to the morning meeting. At that meeting, with all of the department heads, my boss told me that they decided to move me to a different facility in a different job.

Although I had helped save the part of the business that I was managing, they moved me to another part of the business which was now failing. She wanted me to do it again. So here I was, driving over an hour each way to and from work, working for a woman who didn't respect me enough to share my job change with me privately, who was now expecting me to turn around a failing business unit that I have almost no experience with. How did we get to this?

I had been okay with my salary before maternity leave–it wasn't amazing, but it was solid, and I enjoyed my work, so it didn't faze me. Now, I was constantly stressed. I knew I wasn't long for this place. Within three months, I resigned. I took a job that was equivalent pay, a ten-minute commute, and offered me a flexible work arrangement. I was back in the driver seat of my career, and I had two hours of time back into each day, which I quickly reallocated to spend with my family. The money was definitely secondary.

If I think back on it, there was a moment when things turned. It happened when I was pregnant. This was a family business. One day Rae's mother, who was the owner of the company, reviewed our customer satisfaction surveys. She was not happy with some of the results. She berated my boss in front of all of the department heads in the team leader meeting. It was horribly embarrassing. From then on, our environment went from nurturing to militant. I mean right down to no coffee cups or personal items at a nurses' station, or any work station, only in break rooms behind closed doors. This was a total 180. There was no recovery from that moment, for her or for us. The environment was forever changed.

This story really struck me. Not only was Andrea suffering in the environment, so was her boss, Rae. Because her boss had no support, and no one to counter-balance her, things quickly spiraled downward. Andrea, a high performer, felt penalized for her maternity leave and disrespected by Rae and her lack of communication. The unrequested and undesirable job change amplified her negative feelings. Then I thought about Rae. Could you imagine being her? Her boss was also her mother, a double whammy! When things got tough at work, she couldn't share the drama with her mama. Her mama caused the drama at work and offered no support at home.

I didn't have the opportunity to interview Rae, but I can see her choice to move from collaborative to autocratic when the pressure to perform was amplified. This is not uncommon. Even though leadership theories and countless studies prove that collaboration and transparency result in higher-performing, more creative team environments, when stress levels rise, some leaders retreat to a guarded, authoritarian style. This creates a repressed environment for employees. Enter the dreaded "low morale," which is shortly followed by a rise in attrition.

Carla

A different scenario, from my interview with Carla, a therapist in a school district, points to the impact of an employee's immediate supervisor:

> When I first started with this particular district, I had eight years of experience as a speech therapist. The contract I was offered was only paying for five years of experience, but considering full time work, pension, and proximity to home, it was worth the trade-off. Unfortunately, though, the contract steps were frozen for a good number of years and there were no raises and no step movements in the salary guide. Eventually that was straightened out but it was a very minimal salary. At that time, my supervisor was great, the job was close to my house and my kid's school, and I loved my coworkers. Then my supervisor changed. My new supervisor had been a speech therapist prior to becoming an administrator. When she started she repeatedly told the speech therapists under her, five

total, that she understood where we were coming from and what we did.

Gradually as time went on I noticed she would try to get some therapists to admit things about other therapists in their absence. For instance, when Susan was not yet at a meeting, not late just not yet there, she would say so has Susan had more struggles this week? Some of the younger therapists might contribute to the conversation with their assessment of Susan's therapy sessions. All the while, when this supervisor observed Susan during the year, she would get acceptable reviews. She was never offered an action plan to help her become a better therapist, but still our supervisor would encourage covert "attacks" through our colleagues. This supervisor also rearranged a colleague's office because she didn't like the way it was arranged. I'm talking moved desks and filing cabinets in an office that wasn't hers!

In my final review of my time at that district, I again received an exemplary score. Four is perfect, and my score for the year was 3.6. During the review, though, she told me I needed to be more like Mary. She believed that Mary was a leader and that Mary would tell her the ins and out of the department—and then proceeded to tell me second-hand information about the other three speech therapists that I am sure they did not intend her to know. Nothing shared was about them doing a poor job or anything negative about work ethic. Most of the information was the other therapists' dislike for her as a supervisor, including some of my own words that I knew I had said in front of Mary.

This supervisor then told me her opinion of the quality of each of the other four therapists, both her professional opinion and personal. I tried to stop her and actually said, "That's none of my business." She was trying to, it seemed, create an atmosphere of trust and loyalty to her and against my colleagues. Truthfully, I left that review meeting and applied to other jobs on my phone on my way to the car. It felt wrong and sleazy to know these discussions were being held behind closed doors, no matter what side of the door I was on for the discussion. I knew there had to be other times when I was on the outside of a door with a discussion about me happening on the inside.

When I went on interviews, I was never sure it would be better, but I only prayed it couldn't be worse. I ended up taking the job that offered me the most money. I didn't tell the new district that I was leaving the old one due to a supervisor. I told them I wanted to find a place where I could be the therapist I dreamed of being when I was in graduate school. That wasn't a lie; I knew I didn't want to be an employee where people were pitted against each other, where backstabbing and childish behavior occurred from the top down. I know I'll never escape that completely, but I knew I didn't want to work where it was pretty much encouraged.

And so, a competitive school district lost a leading therapist not because of pay, but because of leadership issues. A supervisor exhibited values inconsistent with the school district's values, but it went unchecked. One of the most powerful pieces of this interview with Carla is her comment that upon leaving the meeting where information was shared improperly, she began applying for other jobs. It was immediate. The defining moment where trust no longer existed or could be relied upon was significant enough for her to move on.

Tricia

One final story comes from Jackson, a senior manager in a professional services firm, about an aspiring leader named Tricia.

As a manager in the firm, I see a lot of things. The story that weighs on me the most is this one. We had an employee named Tricia. She had been with the firm for six years. She was by all accounts a rock star. Tricia rose quickly from a junior level staff member to a team lead and manager. She was driving business growth in a critical area of the market. She was strong at developing people, and had been most recently placed in charge of a tough contract where the client didn't want us. She turned it around and made it a growth business, securing option years and additional scope. This was no small feat. She effectively managed a diverse group of staff, including a slate of non-traditional workers, to deliver the full set of services to the customer, and successfully encultured them with our values and work ethic/expectations. Truly, the world was her oyster and she could go as far as she wanted within the firm...

But...(sigh)... Tricia had a different view and values set than her immediate leadership. Her immediate supervisor is also a very successful, long-term employee, but hard-charging in a different way. The boss wasn't a horror show by any means. She was actually very warm personally, but had extremely high expectations of herself and everybody around her, and was not always empathetic when it came to the work. When it has to do with her portfolio, all the warmth goes out the window; she was Type A all the way.

Tricia was an advocate of "servant leadership," and actually gave a presentation on that subject at a division team meeting. That was the turning point... her immediate supervisor and the next level up supervisor responded with an eye roll. There wasn't much respect for the concept. But for Tricia, the notion of servant leadership was very real. She advocated for it and ran her team that way. As time went on, the disconnect between her vision of her path and her values and that of the organization she reported within became evident. The eye rolls never really went away, and I believe that was the moment where she knew she had to do something different. She knew her values and saw that they no longer aligned with the structure she had to operate within if she was to grow her career here.

So often we hear that people leave because they don't see a path: there isn't opportunity or room for mobility. Tricia left because she saw a path and didn't like it. The organization made a decision, conscious or unconscious, that despite the value she brought, it wasn't worth taking the effort to validate and support how she viewed the world, because it didn't match what the bosses thought. As a result, we lost. We lost a top performer capable of managing clients, growing staff, and expanding the business; a diverse point of view at a time when diversity of thought and practice is critical; and an opportunity to show others who have an alternate view about how to motivate people that there is more than one way to be successful. This was a real shame.

This story gave me great pause. It is this, the culture of the eye roll, the dismissive placation of an alternate approach, that is sabotaging otherwise successful leaders. They are successful leading people who are just like them, or who are malleable and willing to become just like them. Varying views and approaches are entertained only as long as they fit within the mold. This leaves little room for innovation, and, in short, works against diversity. There is nothing egregious here, and many times it goes unnoticed. These exits are often re-categorized under the better offer or life-change buckets so as to not have to really examine why a high-performer chose to exit, and not have to rehabilitate incumbent, relatively successful, managers.

Unhealthy Goodbyes – Negative Involuntary Attrition

Terminations happen for a variety of reasons. There are times when a leader chooses to terminate an employee for reasons that are clear only to that leader, and possibly his advocates. Sometimes business costs are too high, sometimes stress is too high, and sometimes it appears to just be easier to let someone go than to identify what changes are needed for successful collaboration. I classify these as the "it seemed like a good idea at the time" separations. By and large, leaders aren't looking to sabotage their businesses. So, they don't take firing an employee, especially a high-performer, lightly. Something has moved them to believe they have no other option. If you are feeling this way, I highly recommend you step away from the situation, go in motion (get physically active) and then seek outside objective counsel. Decisions made from a temporary agitated emotional state are never your best decisions. Anxiety is not your friend, and neither is anger. Calm is the ultimate leadership power, especially when addressing trying employee situations.

Marina

The story below is from an interview with Marina.

In 2009, I was let go from a company that I had worked with for four years. In those four years, I met every goal, never said no, worked in communities from as far south as Town A* (30 miles) and as far north as Town B* (75 miles) for the benefit of the company's eight assisted living communities. I forfeited vacations, time off with family, and my personal life to ensure my facilities *were running smoothly; two of them were start up communities. One thing was constant: I was and continue to be an advocate for the residents I am entrusted to care for. On two occasions, I chose to hold my ground with the owner's brother-in-law, who was the COO at the time. He was lewd, arrogant, and inappropriate, and did not have one ounce of compassion for the clients we served; his only focus was on the bottom line. I was appalled. Our clients are people, and when you need to move assisted living residents, you are moving their long-term homes, their personal items, their lives. This is a very different situation than moving a short-term rehab patient or hospital patient from one building to another or one wing to another.*

I learned over time that the company did not value their employees, but instead created a culture by which the owner (CEO) and the COO felt we as employees should feel honored and appreciative that we were lucky enough to be employed by them, rather than they being proud and lucky to have such good and devoted employees.

About four months after my last disagreement with the COO, I had a meeting with my regional director on a Thursday morning. He told me, "I think it's best if we part ways." And that was it; he gave me no reason, just told me to pack up and walked me out. Never anything even close to a write-up; my record was nothing but meeting or exceeding goal after goal. And yet, I was asked to leave. Not only was I offered no severance, I wasn't even paid for Friday! I lost almost two months of accrued vacation time... and nothing... that is how I was treated. "At-will employee" means I work as long as it's their will, I guess. This was a defining moment for me in my career. I came to realize that everyone is replaceable. At any moment, things can change. From that moment on, I decided that I would always take time for myself and counsel others to do the same. Work will always be there.

Here's the kicker—no, really, you won't believe this. Three years later, I get a call from the head of HR from the company that fired me asking me, "What would it take to get you to come back?" She didn't even know I was fired. That is nowhere in the records. She identified my file as a high-performer that "got away," and they were hoping they could entice me to rejoin the firm. Once I picked my jaw up off the floor, I told them that I have integrity and that no amount of money would ever give them the "me" they let go, back. So the answer was an unwavering "no, thank you."

After listening to this story I thought, I bet that COO wished he had a "do-over" card to play. It seemed to me that the heat of the moment never got defused and he carried an uncomfortable grudge around with him. When the opportunity arose to enact a termination, he did so, and in a cowardly fashion, sent another leader to deliver the message. Later, when profits fell even further, and he couldn't find another manager as efficient as Marina, he sent HR to woo her back. He had no idea of the impact of his previous decision. He was removing an annoyance from his environment (perceived low impact), when in reality, he was dramatically impacting business operations.

We all make mistakes. If you haven't made any, you aren't being honest with yourself. Look again. Mistakes are how we learn. The bottom line to this is:

"You either get bitter or you get better. It's that simple. You either take what has been dealt to you and allow it to make you a better person, or you allow it to tear you down. The choice does not belong to fate, it belongs to you."
JOSH SHIPP

REFLECTION POINT:
Your Kind of Goodbye

✓ What staff departure keeps you up at night?

_____

_____

_____

✓ What type of attrition has your team experienced?

_____

_____

_____

✓ What situation do you wish you had a "do-over" card for?

_____

_____

_____

✓ What wish do you have for your team and the inevitable future goodbyes?

_____

_____

_____

CHAPTER 3:

Organizational Identity: Values and Org Structure

et's talk about you and your values. It is important to start with your values, because you are the founder of this business, and whether you realize it or not, it is patterned after you. Much like a child shares his or her parents' DNA, your business shares your DNA. You built this business to solve a problem and deliver a service. You also built it so that you could run it. Its structure and processes were designed to your preferences. Whether they remain aligned to your preferences or not, is a choice you will need to make as a leader. But we're not there yet.

REFLECTION POINT:

Personal Values Exercise

Below is a list of values. Take a few minutes to review these values and select the top five in your life. What are the five values that are paramount and non-negotiable for you?

Authenticity	Achievement	Adventure
Authority	Autonomy	Balance
Community	Collaboration	Compentency
Compassion	Challenge	Citizenship
Creativity	Curiosity	Diversity
Empathy	Presence	Wellness
Energy	Entrepreneurship	Excellence
Fairness	Faith	Family
Fun	Grace	Growth
Generosity	Quality	Timeliness
Happiness	Health	Honesty
Humor	Integrity	Justice
Kindness	Leadership	Love
Loyalty	Optimism	Peace

Pleasure	Professionalism	Recognition
Relationships	Respect	Responsibility
Revenue	Safety	Security
Routine	Greed	Frugality
Self-Respect	Service	Strength
Speed	Spirituality	Success
Teamwork	Tenderness	Trust
Victory	Wealth	Wisdom

Top Five Non-Negotiable Values In My Life

1. _____

_____

2. _____

_____

3. _____

_____

4. _____

_____

5. _____

_____

Now take a few minutes, and for each of the values you identified write down how you operationalize each of those in your life. Operationalizing values means how you LIVE the value; what are the real choices you make every day that honor your value as a priority and way of life? Write these operationalization statements in the affirmative – what you DO.

Here's an example.

Value: Family.

Operationalization: I operationalize (LIVE) my value of family by: eating dinner with my daughter every night, performing a consistent bedtime routine, calling each family member and singing happy birthday to them on their birthdays, traveling to be with our extended family every Thanksgiving, Christmas, and Easter, accepting business travel that does not exceed four nights away from home in a row.

Now, your turn. Use the space below to revisit the list of your top five values and describe how you operationalize each one of them in your life.

Value 1: _____

_____

Operationalization: _____

_____

_____

Value 2: _____

_____

Operationalization: _____

_____

_____

Value 3: _____

_____

Operationalization: _____

_____

_____

Value 4: _____

_____

Operationalization: _____

_____

_____

Value 5: _____

_____

Operationalization: _____

_____

_____

Now let's flip it.

What values do you reject? Even if it they are not on the list above–what is something you refuse to allow into your life? How do you reject them in your life?

Top Five Values I Reject in My Life

1. _____

   _____

2. _____

   _____

3. _____

   _____

4. _____

   _____

5. _____

   _____

Here's an example.

Value: Frugality

Rejection: This is a value that I reject in its extreme. I'm happy to use a coupon or wait for a sale on a big-ticket item. I do however reject the value of frugality when it would require me to compromise my values of quality or timeliness. For example, my daughter requested "Chipwich" ice cream treats for her classmates. That purchase was $30. We could have selected Dixie Cup ice cream for $7, less than 25% of the cost of the Chipwiches. But, I had already promised the Chipwich ice cream, as it is her favorite, and she had promised her classmates that special treat. Here I rejected frugality because it would have meant sacrificing on quality. So, Chipwiches are what we bought.

Value 1: _____

_____

Rejection: _____

_____

_____

Value 2: _____

_____

Rejection: _____

_____

_____

Value 3: _____

_____

Rejection: _____

_____

_____

Value 4: _____

_____

Rejection: _____

_____

_____

Value 5: _____

_____

Rejection: _____

_____

_____

REFLECTION POINT:

Business Values Exercise

Let's talk about your business values.

Do you have a mission statement?   If so, write it here.

_____

Do you have a set of organizational values? If so, write them here.

_____

_____

_____

Those words can be used for the exercise below.

If you don't have a mission statement or a list of organizational values, let's review the same list of values and identify the top five that you believe guide your organization.

For each of the five values selected, or for however many you have stated in your organization values list, write an example of how your organization operationalizes the value.

Remember that your operationalization should include the decisions you make, the practices you keep, the interactions you have with clients and staff, and the way work gets distributed and accomplished. What behaviors and events would I see if I were to visit your team that would show me the values of your organization?

Value 1:   _____

_____

Operationalization: _____

_____

_____

Value 2: _____

_____

Operationalization: _____

_____

_____

Value 3: _____

_____

Operationalization: _____

_____

_____

Value 4: _____

_____

Operationalization: _____

_____

_____

Value 5: _____

_____

Operationalization: _____

_____

_____

Now let's flip it.

What values does your corporation reject? How do you operationalize the rejection?

Value 1: _____

_____

Rejection: _____

_____

_____

Value 2: _____

_____

Rejection: _____

_____

_____

Value 3: _____

_____

Rejection: _____

_____

_____

Value 4: _____

_____

Rejection: _____

_____

_____

Value 5: _____

_____

Rejection: _____

_____

_____

REFLECTION POINT:

Values Comparison

Compare your list of personal values with your list of corporate values.

✓ List those that are the same.

_____

_____

_____

✓ List those that are only personal.

_____

_____

_____

✓ List those that are only corporate.

_____

_____

_____

✓ As you reflect on these values, ask yourself if there are any are missing? If so, write them now.

_____

_____

_____

✓ Is there a value that you see rising in importance that hasn't made your list yet?

_____

_____

_____

✓ Are there values that are waning in importance?

_____

_____

_____

✓ How does your business language express a set of values?

_____

_____

_____

✓ To what extent is the senior/management team aligned with and operationalizing them?

_____

_____

_____

It is important to look at the similarities and differences in your Personal and Business Values. Are you showing up the same way in your non-work life and in your work life? Are you holding team members to a set of values that you don't personally embody? Or is it all simpatico?

Organizational Culture

The importance of being clear and clean on your values cannot be overstated. These will drive your organizational culture and therefore your operational norms and decision making.

What is organizational culture? The working definition I use is values in action. Culture is the operationalization of your values, the behavioral norms of an organization. They include how you approach situations, how you engage with each other, and what the default reactions to situations are. Organizational culture can be evidenced in many aspects of organizational life. Here are a few examples:

- Work Location: Is there a campus, a corporate HQ, is it a small biz run out of someone's home? Is work done remotely–each employee in a different place–or are you co-located with customers/clients?
- Dress Code: What do people wear to work–uniforms, suits, business casual, jeans, or maybe even slippers and pjs?
- Work Hours: Do people work standard business hours, weekdays, weekends, 24/7, or anytime they want as long as the work gets done?
- Work Style: How does work get done–team-based assignments, individual contributors, assigned workflow, or project teams?
- Free Time/Breaks: How do team members spend their lunch hours, if they even take their lunch hours? Are there breaks built into the day? If you work co-located is there a place to gather during break times?
- Team Relationships: Do team members create and maintain relationships with colleagues for business purposes only, or do they also engage socially? Are there events? Are families invited?

At the heart of culture is values. What an organization values is what will grow. So, being absolutely clear on your values is what will drive the evolution of your corporate culture. Some of these will be hallmarks, evergreens in your garden. For one organization I work with, it's ethics. They have a deep-seated belief and value in ethical behavior and decision making. The cornerstone of their corporate culture is "ethics."

What does it look like when ethics takes the driver's seat? In this organization. it manifested in open communication, specifically inviting questions from all staff at any time, non-retaliation, and zero tolerance for those who didn't uphold the policies and procedures put in place to ensure above-board operations. Sometimes that meant the exiting of "rain-makers." Why would an organization let go a top salesperson? Isn't business about making money? The answer for this organization was that as important as sales and revenue were, it came second to maintaining their standards and upholding their values. No sale was worth compromising their values and their integrity. When an organization's leaders apply their values consistently in their business management and decision making, it reinforces the org culture and sends a strong message to all employees. This is who we are and what we believe, and we will protect that at all costs.

Organizational culture is not static. An organization is comprised of people who live and learn and grow every day. As those people change and adapt their work processes and interactions, the organization changes along with them. Culture evolves.

Sometimes we want to evolve it on purpose! Planned and purposeful evolution of culture is more than ok, it's a sign of life and growth. The question to ask is: are our values evolving, or are we choosing to operationalize them in a different way? Either answer is fine; the important piece here is pausing to ask that question and consciously choosing the evolution.

REFLECTION POINT:

Culture Check

Consider answering these questions yourself and asking them of your team. Compare the answers:

✓ What is the best part of our team culture?

_____

_____

_____

✓ What, if any, part of our culture feels like it might not be in alignment with the rest of our business?

_____

_____

_____

✓ What would you say makes our team strong?

_____

_____

_____

✓ What is your experience as a contributor to the team?

_____

_____

_____

✓ What is your favorite part of how we operate?

_____

_____

_____

✓ If you had a magic wand, what would you change?

_____

_____

_____

✓ What is the most exciting part about working on this team?

_____

_____

_____

✓ What, if any, challenges keep you up at night?

_____

_____

_____

From Game to Garden

Perhaps the best visual I can offer you in regard to organizational culture when it is not consciously crafted and protected is Jenga®. Jenga is a favorite game in my family, and I think it fits very well here. Every time you allow an unplanned or un-architected change in your organizational operations or values, you pull a piece from the culture (Jenga) tower, and with each addition of a new behavior or an unintended re-prioritization of values, you put a piece on the top of the (Jenga) tower. If you pull too many pieces, or don't balance correctly when adding to the top, the tower tumbles.

As these pieces are pulled and others are added to the top, the tower gets wobbly and unstable. The first few likely go almost unnoticed, as the structure is solid and the supports around the holes are strong. But as you keep going, anxiety rises. As mentioned earlier, in times of anxiety or organizational stress, two behaviors surface: over-performance and under-performance.

In Jenga, these two types appear as well. The over-performer gets excited and hyper, testing the stability of all the pieces, planning which ones should be moved next, offering unsolicited advice to other players, raising their anxiety even higher. The under-performers are the ones who barely breathe near the tower. They want to skip their turn and hope that if the tower falls it is on someone else's turn. They watch carefully and when forced to make a move, they base it on information gathered from watching the other players. This goes round after round until the tower tumbles. You see, there is no winning in Jenga. There is surviving for as long as you can, until it's over. The game ends at the same time for everyone, at the point of collapse.

It is absolutely possible to recover from a tumbled tower–you rebuild it and start again. The rebuilding can be time consuming, depending on how many people help. Some players jump right in and begin aligning and stacking pieces quickly, excited to get going again. Other players decide to opt out of the rebuilding or to opt out of the game all together. This game is not for everyone. Some players just can't bear the idea that a piece of the puzzle tower may land in their drink or spill onto their laps or crash onto the floor, drawing attention to the group. You can also be sure that nobody wants to be responsible for making it fall again, either.

So, if your tower tumbles, as the CEO, it's your job to own it, pick up the pieces, and build again.

Is it possible to prevent the tower from tumbling? Absolutely. Don't play a game with your culture. There is no winning or losing–there is only losing. The Jenga tower always tumbles. Change your mental model of your culture. Leave the gaming behind and treat your organization as a garden. Then tend it and it will grow. When planting the seeds, you have to determine the right seeds to plant and the right time to plant them, and then care for them. Ensure the seeds have ample sun and water and are protected from the animals that wander by looking for food. Pull the weeds regularly. You can grow a beautiful garden, as long as you spend time as the gardener.

CHAPTER 4:

Finding the Right Talent: The Power of Passion

"You'll attract the employees you need if you can explain why your mission is compelling: not why it's important in general, but why you're doing something important that no one else is going to get done."

PETER THIEL

arlier in the book, I asked you to remember Employee #1—your first team member. They likely joined your team because you knew them; you were somehow connected already, as colleagues, friends, or they were referred from a trusted source. Your first invitation to join your team and share in the life of your creation was someone who came with referrals.

The flip side of this equation is also true—you were not a stranger. Employee #1 had a relationship with you and trusted that you had a viable, brilliant idea for a business that they wanted to join. Why? Likely because of you. Because you were going to offer something new and in a new way. There was no other organization that was doing what you were doing or how you were doing it. This was really new, groundbreaking. Excitement and prestige accompany being on the ground floor of a new initiative. Anyone can be successful executing a proven method. Not everyone can architect a new vision and breathe life into it. That's special.

So your initial recruiting was probably a hybrid of an investing strategy and a staffing plan. You had no HR director or Chief of Staff to draw an organization plan, identify key skills and abilities, and envision a workflow. No, you had yourself, your computer, and a passionate, clear vision of a service you and only you could provide your way. Then, you realized you couldn't do it alone, so you carefully selected the tasks you could comfortably allow someone else to do.

REFLECTION POINT:
Hiring Employee #1

✓ What did you look for when finding employee #1?

_____

_____

_____

✓ What were the most important qualities for him/her to have?

_____

_____

_____

✓ What story did you tell to explain your vision and how he/she would be a part of it?

_____

_____

_____

✓ What was your dream and hope for him/her joining your team?

_____

_____

_____

✓ What was your expectation of how work would happen?

_____

_____

_____

✓ Now... think about today. If you were recruiting, how would you answer the last four questions?

_____

_____

_____

✓ What pieces are the same? What pieces have evolved?

_____

_____

_____

Surely some pieces are the same, unless you have changed your business entirely. I'm working on the assumption that you have not. If you launched an interior design business, you're still running an interior design business, not a childcare center or a publishing house. Therefore your business has maintained its original industry purpose. What may be different? Perhaps you have gotten more specialized in your products/ services, or perhaps you have branched out and now offer a family of products/services. Maybe you started delivering individual services and now work with groups. Inevitably, if your business has not only survived but grown, change occurred. You hired more team members and built an organization. Your interest now is in keeping them. Great, so why am I writing to you about recruiting?

Recruiting is foundational to your organization; it is a future employee's first experience with you as an employer. Sure, they may know you or know of you in another context, but your role and relationship with them as employer/employee will be different. A discussion between friends is not the same discussion that happens between a business owner and an employee. Back to the small business as a family analogy–you are the Parent, the alpha. There is a power dynamic, and instead of wasting time trying to disprove it, you are much better served identifying and defining it, and determining the best way to work within it.

There was a time, prior to the dawn of the internet, when potential employees carefully crafted resumes and detailed cover letters to specifically and passionately communicate their interest in learning about joining an organization. Candidates would visit their local stationery store and sensibly select the perfect linen stationery and matching envelopes to print their letters and mail them off with a wish and a hope.

The recruiting side of this scenario was basically ads in the newspaper, a recruiting team that would receive incoming resumes, possibly an employee referral system, and the reliable stand-by, on-campus recruiting, for new graduates just entering the workforce. Senior jobs were staffed by head hunters.

The dynamic at that time meant that potential employees hustled, and employers received. One might argue that the dynamic favored the employer. In terms of energy spent, that would be true. But did they always get the best, most qualified, most diverse candidates? No. They got the ones that came to them, who knew how to work the system.

Then came the Internet. Job searching went from scouring the *Washington Post* employment section to posting an electronic resume and searching various job boards for potential positions. Monster. com seemed to be the definitive job matching site. Soon after that, the electronic want ads diversified, and then specialized. Specialized sites for various industries came into play, professional organizations and universities became even more active in helping place their members/ students. Activity increased. Applying for jobs became as easy as a few mouse clicks and an email. The numbers of resumes received continued to increase. Somehow, this felt like the playing field was leveling. Potential employees had more avenues, more visibility, and more opportunity to be seen and to reach into businesses they wanted to join. Organizations had a fuller, more diverse pool of candidates. This felt a little more like match-making than blind dates.

Continue forward to today. The various online applications still exist, but now recruiters are reaching out into networks searching for candidates. LinkedIn and other social media platforms are scanned daily, searched with keywords, skills, interests, and networks, to find people who look and sound like current successful employees of the business. The relationship aspect plays a larger role, an individual's network is almost as important as their individual qualities and qualifications.

What about on the organization side? The same is true: potential employees scan to see who is already employed there, and research them, while questioning—is that a group I want to belong to? Potential employees also research products/services and customer satisfaction. Everyone wants to be proud of where they work. The power of prestige plays a significant role in recruiting. This means an organizations' reputation must be stellar, comprised of brilliant leaders; ethical, smart, fun employees; satisfied customers; and top-notch products. This also means that social media presence must reflect that level of excellence as well. It is here that marketing and recruiting become one and the same. Recruiting is the courtship of your first customers–your employees. Recruiting has transitioned from an organization giving an employee a chance to prove himself to an organization presenting itself in the most honest and positive way to attract candidates to apply. The dynamic has once again changed.

Recruiting methods have also evolved. While applications continue to be part of the recruitment process, they no longer hold the same weight. Recruiting happens in much more social settings. Aside from networking and referrals and on-line introductions through social media and other platforms, many recruiting activities happen without being framed as recruiting. Potential employers sponsor events, participate in industry events, and host competitions with prizes (i.e., hackathons) where top talent go to meet others, and or participate for the fun of it or the competition aspect. These settings are important because they offer interaction with people in an informal way, without sacrificing the opportunity to show functional skill and ability. For employers, they allow a glimpse into how potential employees think, act, work, and problem-solve. For potential employees, it offers an opportunity to interact with current employees and leaders, and get a feel for their culture.

Why does this matter? Isn't a job a job? No. Potential employees seek way more than a job and a paycheck. They are seeking an experience, a place to belong, to be challenged, to grow, to learn, and to laugh. The work is important, yes, but it is not enough. The pay must be competitive and fair, but that is not enough either. Employees today are seeking an overall lifestyle fit. They want to be with people who encourage them to be their best selves and who support their places in the world. Hmmm–sounds like a second family, doesn't it?

- 85% of new professionals/soon-to-be college graduates said employee treatment and welfare were what they look for in future employers (Nielsen)
- 86% of new professionals/soon-to-be college graduates say it's important that the company they work for behaves in a socially responsible way (Nielsen)

In order to effectively recruit staff into your organization, you must have a clear, articulated, documented value proposition for them. Yes, clear work expectations are a must, as is fair pay–but as the saying goes, those are table stakes. Every organization offers a good job description, and reputable organizations offer fair wages. What will attract the right top talent to your organization is the description of the employee experience. What will someone's life be like working with you and your team?

The Surprise Offer

Reggie had a great job. He had a manager he trusted, he had been promoted twice in the last five years, and his pay was above average for his years of experience. Further, he was regularly offered enrichment opportunities, including travel. He was generally happy. Reggie was, however, considering a relocation. He had been living in the area for over 10 years, and since he had no family ties to the area, he thought now was a good time to look around. He casually floated his resume to a few places in the new location just to see what was out there.

Within just a few days, he received a call from a recruiter. Before he knew it, a phone screen was underway, and then they were asking to set him up with a series of interviews. This was easy, and actually kind of fun. Reggie participated in the interviews, which were largely unstructured. The CEO had already reviewed Reggie's resume and was satisfied with his bona fides, and used this time to volley ideas and explore topics of mutual interest. Reggie sensed he would get an offer when the CEO said to him, "You know, I like you." And the interview wrapped. Two days later, Reggie's phone rang. It was the CEO offering him the job. He asked him to accept the job then, and start the following week–not even allowing two weeks to close up at his current job.

Reggie met with his coach to discuss the situation. The offer was strong (financially competitive), exciting (a more senior position), and would allow for paid relocation whenever Reggie wanted to move. So, what was holding him back? The CEO wanted an answer on the spot. Reggie politely said he couldn't answer that quickly but would get back to him within two days.

Ultimately, Reggie turned down the offer. Why? Because the urgency the CEO met him with was a sign that the company had a culture of high-pressure, fast decision-making, and low regard for boundaries. The call for the phone screen, the interview set-up, and then the offer were all delivered very quickly... maybe too quickly. There was a high-pressure, sales-y feel to it that Reggie didn't like. There was also no regard for the fact that he was currently employed and had commitments to uphold. In fact, when he envisioned making the call to decline the job, he imagined the CEO applying more pressure. This was not the environment or the culture Reggie wanted to join. As energetic and exciting as the CEO was, he wasn't the type of leader or manager Reggie wanted to work for. His recruiting experience gave him a window in to this firm, and while the work was a match, the culture was not.

Let's take a few minutes and reflect on your firm's recruiting experience.

REFLECTION POINT:

Recruiting Experience

✓ How do you source your candidates? Who does this?

_____

_____

_____

✓ What style of interview do you use to screen
candidates? Who conducts the interview if not you?

_____

_____

_____

✓ What do you spend your interview time talking with
candidates about?

_____

_____

_____

✓ What do you want candidates to experience when they
meet with you/your team?

_____

_____

_____

✓ What are the top five descriptor words you use when
describing your company?

_____

_____

_____

✓ What are the descriptor words you use when
describing the candidates you seek?

_____

_____

_____

✓ How do the candidates you ultimately hire describe themselves?

_____

_____

_____

✓ What are your stories of service?

_____

_____

_____

✓ What do you need to hear to know someone is a fit for your team?

_____

_____

_____

✓ What feeling do you hope your recruiting process generates?

_____

_____

_____

Take a moment and flip back to the Values exercise. With those values in mind, re-read your recruiting process. Does your process operationalize your personal values and/or your business values? If it does, then it is more likely that you enjoy the recruiting process and sense that the candidates you receive and ultimately hire are good fits for your firm. If not, it is more likely that you are frustrated with the recruiting process and it feels difficult to find the right hires.

If your recruiting process is a good reflection of your values, keep going with it! If it isn't, this is a good process to revise. Once you re-design this process, you will experience an improved talent pool flowing through the sourcing and interviewing pipeline. These candidates will likely be a better fit with your organizational culture. When you increase the quality of your hires, you take the first step to increasing the productivity of your team as well as increasing your overall retention.

CHAPTER 5:

Delivering for a Higher Purpose: Organization as Community

*"When people go to work, they shouldn't have to
leave their hearts at home."*
BETTY BENDER

Your organization is built, you've hired your team, now your job is to build and nurture the community. Community has two meanings here: 1) the community of your organization, and 2) the larger community of which your organization is a member. I used the word ecosystem earlier to describe what you were building, and it holds true. Your organization is an ecosystem within a larger ecosystem. Your job is to feed it and ensure it remains pollution-free.

Organizational Community

Let's first discuss the community of your organization, the community that is your business. Research shows that employees of all generations, not just millennials, are seeking a holistic employment experience. This is far different than the days of a "job." Today, employees view their corporate communities as just that: a community, a family, a home away from home. There is a great need to belong and to be a part of something special. As Shawn Anchor writes in *The Happiness Advantage*, "The fastest way to disengage an employee is to tell him his work is meaningful only because of the paycheck."

Enter the term "employee engagement." I'm certain you've heard this term and have likely been told you need to invest in it in order to maintain your business. I won't disagree, as employee engagement is fundamentally important. I do take issue with the fact that it has somehow devolved into something organizations do to employees, a shorthand for corporate programs that employees can attend. That is not employee engagement. Industry has framed employee engagement as primarily a one-way push from organization to employee. That really is only half of the equation. Yes, organizations must offer a framework and opportunities for employees to plug into, but it is not solely to receive. These opportunities are only helpful and relevant if employees choose to show up and also make requests of the organization for themselves. To engage employees, you must build an emotional connection between employees and their work, and between employees and their community, realized through shared experiences. Executive business coach Marshall Goldsmith refers to this as an equation in which 50% of the effort belongs to the organization, and 50% of it belongs to the employee. Studies have been conducted to assess the impact of engagement. Let's look at a few of those findings:

According to the Temkin Group, highly engaged employees are:

- 2.5 times more likely to stay at work late if something needs to be done after the normal workday ends
- more than twice as likely to help someone at work even if they don't ask for help
- more than three times as likely to do something good for the company that is not expected of them
- more than five times as likely to recommend that a friend or relative apply for a job at their company

Can you relate to that? Have you ever stayed late or offered to help out on something without being asked? I know I have. Have you referred friends or family into an organization where you worked? I have done that as well. Why does this happen? Because you are connected and committed to the organization, the people, the work, the mission, and the customers. It feels like the right thing to do. This is the type of community you want to build in your organization if you hope to attract and retain top talent. This is a community that contributes.

"When people are financially invested, they want a return. When people are emotionally invested, they want to contribute."
SIMON SINEK

Mary

Mary is a senior manager who distributes her time between three customer project teams and an internal project team. She also mentors about eight people within her firm. She is upbeat, and describes herself as people-focused. Mary is the kind of manager who always finds time to meet with anyone who needs support, and because of that, when she asks for volunteers, she quickly gets raised hands. She is also happy to take on any task that needs doing, in support of others. She has built a culture of teamwork and a reputation for collaboration. In fact, her teams like to call themselves the GID crew (Get It Done). They even made coffee mugs with a GID logo. Mary is regarded by many as a role model. When I interviewed Mary, she didn't seem to realize the impact she had on the larger team. She knew she was happy and her teams were happy, and regarded how she worked as nothing special, just doing her thing.

As a project manager, Mary coordinates the work of several task managers and relies on them to handle daily task execution. She spoke so highly of those task managers, describing them as "superstars," and guessed she would "be working for them one day." She knew about each of them: who had children, who had applications in for graduate school, who was traveling overseas for their next vacation. It was evident that she felt invested in their careers and their personal success and happiness. You won't be surprised to hear that Mary had the lowest turnover in the company and the highest customer satisfaction ratings.

When employees are engaged and part of a corporate community, another level of magic happens. It is the kind of magic that exists within Mary's team. Gallup researched and presented the findings below.

Employees who are engaged and have high well-being are:
- 42% more likely to evaluate their overall lives highly
- 27% more likely to report "excellent" performance in their own job at work
- 27% more likely to report "excellent" performance by their organization
- 45% more likely to report high levels of adaptability in the presence of change
- 37% more likely to report always recovering "fully" after illness, injury, or hardship
- 59% less likely to look for a job with a different organization in the next 12 months

- 18% less likely to change employers in a 12-month period
- 19% more likely to volunteer their time in the past month.

Patty

A friend of mine moved from one firm to another. She was happy with her move, and so I asked her, what do you like the most, what's the biggest difference? Her answer was not more money, better benefits, more flexibility, a better boss, or more interesting work. Her answer was simply: "They say, 'thank you.' Literally, people thank me for what I do, for taking time, for showing up. I hadn't realized that we didn't thank each other at my old job, until I noticed people thanking me at my new job. It really makes a difference."

What Patty was telling me was that not only was she engaged, but her engagement was appreciated. Not only were the leaders she was working with appreciative, but so were her peers and direct reports, and they made it a priority to say so. The culture of the organization she joined was operationalizing their value of engagement by consistently expressing gratitude and appreciation for it. This culture also clearly valued gratitude because they lived it. This operationalization of the value made a huge difference, and Patty felt it. Gratitude is a builder of all relationships. Just as you would thank a friend for listening to you, or a sibling for a birthday present, you should thank the people you work with for their contributions to your shared experiences. Gratitude is also addictive, much like happiness. The more you practice it, the more you experience it.

"Everyone wants to be appreciated, so if you appreciate someone, don't keep it a secret."

MARY KAY ASH, FOUNDER OF MARY KAY COSMETICS

REFLECTION POINT:
Gratitude Practices at Work

Take a few minutes and read the following Gratitude Practices. Select one that you will implement this week.

Make the commitment to yourself and your team to this practice, and block time on your calendar to do it.

While you are in your calendar, reserve time two weeks from now to review this list again, and repeat the process.

At the end of the week, spend 10 minutes journaling about the practice: how you felt, what you thought about, what you will do differently next week.

- ✓ Say "thank you": make it specific (thank you for...). Practice this daily until it becomes your habit.
- ✓ Gratitude cards: once a month, write a card to a team member expressing your gratitude for who they are on the team, and what a difference they make to you and the environment.
- ✓ Team appreciation lunch: host a team appreciation lunch and when inviting the team, give each person cards (one for each other team member), with the instruction to write a note of gratitude on the card. (i.e., for Carole: Carole, I am grateful for the humor you bring to our meetings, you always know when we need to lighten up. For Tom: Tom, I'm grateful for your punctuality–you keep us on track and don't let us lose focus during meetings. For Anne: Anne, I'm grateful for your creativity, the idea to use mind-mapping to

solve the problem last week was awesome, etc.) At the lunch, distribute the stack of cards to each team member. Invite them to read them aloud.

✓ Anniversary celebrations: your team members choose to work for you. Every anniversary is an important one, not just the milestones in five-year increments. Every year someone chooses to be part of your team is a choice to spend another year of his/her life with you. Celebrate that! Take him/her to lunch. Write a note of appreciation, and in it, be purposeful, meaningful, and genuine in your expression of gratitude for the investment in the team.

"Highly engaged employees make the customer experience. Disengaged employees break it."
TIMOTHY R. CLARK

The Greater Community

Being a good corporate citizen, a responsible member of the community, is good for business. We know this as nearly all large organizations have either a volunteer corps, or a corporate social responsibility committee. Organizations receive accolades for their volunteer service and for their impact on the greater community. Research finds that volunteerism is also a path for the development of critical job skills. If there aren't enough opportunities to develop a skill in a paid position, volunteering often offers the opportunity to learn while serving. Beyond that, it feels good to contribute to the greater good. The Millennial generation is acutely focused on contribution to the betterment of overall society, perhaps even more so than any previous generation. They are highly networked, online constantly, and have been socialized to crowdsource analysis of difficult issues as well as fundraise for local and large initiatives. There is an expectation that all of us are citizens of the world, and employers are held to the same standard to be active contributors. In the 1980s, we heard "Greed is good." Today it is all about contributing to the greater good. Leave the world a better place than when you found it.

- 84% of millennials say that helping to make a positive difference in the world is more important than professional recognition (Bentley University)
- 82% of millennials said it was important to them to have a career that does some good in the world (Clark University)
- 63% of millennials like their employers to contribute to social or ethical causes (Brookings)

Practically speaking, what does that mean? The more your organization puts good into the world, the more engaged your employees will be. This ties directly back to your desire to serve. If you are serving your clients, you are meeting them where they are and helping them move to a better place. By providing your product/service, you are responding to a need, and your delivery is adding to the greater good. This is something to be proud of. Further, your organization is a business, so it is for-profit. You have the ability to make donations of either revenue or goods or time or service to support external not-for-profits. This is one of the ways you can build the community, and be a good neighbor to others.

Businesses with high retention are devoted to their communities. They identify non-profits or causes that are in alignment with their values and they actively support them. A friend of mine runs a successful business coaching runners. Twice a year, she hosts events that generate profits, which are donated to Girls on the Run. These events always sell out. Her customers believe in active lifestyles and believe in encouraging girls to live strong, healthy lives, so they happily contribute to this cause. The same goes for her employees and business partners. They proudly promote these events and share them on their social media. Hundreds of pictures are posted, thousands of dollars raised and donated, and the relationship her business has with her customers and team is strengthened; the engagement is palpable.

Another way to contribute to the greater good is by following the lead of your team. You hired the best and the brightest to join your business. Your team is highly networked, highly aware, and active in their communities. Each person on your team has something they believe in. Whether they volunteer at the animal shelter on weekends, participate in Relay for Life to raise money for the American Cancer Society, spend their free time as a troop leader at Girl or Boy Scouts, or serve at the soup kitchen on holidays, they are out there contributing their time and talent to support the greater good. All you need to do is listen. As you listen to what matters to them and where they invest, you will hear that each team member is offering you an opportunity to serve. They are presenting to you the opportunity to join them in serving the greater good.

What would happen if you asked each one of your team members to present their favorite non-profit/service opportunity to the whole team, and invited them to all join in and support? What do you think would happen in that moment where your entire team chose to follow the lead of a colleague and support the greater good? I'll give you a hint: magic. Everyday magic is what happens here. First, you are putting a team member in the role of leader, and publicly recognizing it. They are growing new skills and feeling what it is to stand in their own power and lead. Second, you are happily taking the role of follower, which is a healthy exercise and powerful not only for you, but for your team.

Third, you are 100% in service to others. This, simply put, feels good. It feels good to be doing something for the good of others, for the pure reason of being kind. Last and certainly not least, you are investing in the hearts of your people. You are building the relationships you have with them, the ones they have with each other, and the relationship your business has within the community. The bottom-line take-away to this section is this: if you are making all the decisions, including what external organizations to support, you are missing a huge opportunity to engage with your team and your community. Invite your team to lead the way here. Follow their lead on where to invest in the community. This will empower them, and open doors for you and your business.

REFLECTION POINT:
Contributing to the Greater Good

✓ What charitable contributions does your business make every year? monetary/goods? time/service?

_____

_____

_____

✓ What role does your team play in these contributions?

_____

_____

_____

✓ Set a goal to double your contributions this year and share that goal with your team. Solicit ideas on how you could meet that goal as a team.

✓ Be open, and commit to support.

Now, get out of the way, and watch magic happen.

CHAPTER 6:

Keeping the Top Talent & Maintaining Organizational Health

"Paychecks can't buy passion."
BRAD FEDERMAN

L et's review for a moment where we have been so far on this journey together. You boldly put your dream into action and stood up a business. You took on the role of leader and invited others to join you in making your vision a reality. You lost some people along the way. You paused and took stock of your values and did a check-in to make sure those values are operationalized in the way you live and lead. You assessed your recruiting to ensure you are tapping into the right talent and growing your team in a healthy way. You know, and I mean you really completely know, that your team is here for an experience, not a paycheck. Working with you, on your team, is an investment and is frankly their home away from home. Who you are, how you behave, what you do–it all matters to them, as does the quality of work they do and the good they add into the world.

Now we are going to look at a few key areas that are critical to your business health and to maintaining your top talent. Because let's get to the point here–if you are not willing to do it, someone else is. The biggest asset of any business is its people. The businesses that keep the top people are the ones taking time to walk their talk and invest where it matters. So, where is that investment being made: 1) Quality of Management/Leadership, 2) Career Path/ Professional Growth, and/or 3) Workplace Environment?

As a side note, I won't be delving into pay or benefits in this book. I believe it goes without saying that not only fair, but competitive, wages are table stakes, and benefits packages are part of overall compensation. There are many, robust studies on compensation that you can review, but I honestly believe you already know what a competitive benefits and pay plan looks like. Your choice is simple: offer it and attract talent, or don't.

Quality of Management/Leadership

I'm sure you have heard the saying, people don't leave jobs, they leave managers. While this is not true 100% of the time–not everyone leaves because they had a poor manager–it is statistically the front-runner of cause for attrition. Everyone wants to have someone who is looking out for them, who appreciates them, and who truly is working to ensure their experience is a good one. This goes right back to my assertion in the Introduction that your job managing people is different from your job running the business. Your people are your most valuable asset. They are what make your business run. If they don't feel that their management/leadership has their best interests at heart, they will be disengaged. There is no engagement if there is no relationship.

- The main factor in workplace discontent is not wages, benefits, or hours, but the boss (Gallup)
- Managers account for at least 70% of variance in employee engagement scores (Gallup)
- 50% of U.S. adults have left their job to get away from their manager (Gallup)
- 28% of employees would rather have a better boss than a $5,000 raise (Randstad)
- 80% of those dissatisfied with their managers are also disengaged from their employers (Dale Carnegie)
- Engagement plummets to 2% among teams with managers who ignore their employees, compared 61% for teams led by managers who focus on strengths (Gallup)

Let's look at the flip side. What happens when employees have an engaged manager, much like Mary, who was described in the previous chapter. Those employees feel connected, supported, and engaged.

- Employees who say they have more supportive supervisors are 1.3 times as likely to stay with the organization and are 67% more engaged (The Energy Project)
- Feeling encouraged by a supervisor to take breaks increases by nearly 100% people's likelihood to stay with any given company, and also doubles their sense of health and well-being (The Energy Project)

How do we build this connectivity? The same way we build any other relationship; by showing up, listening, and keeping our word. That sounds simple doesn't it? It is simple, but it is a dance. You have a symbiotic relationship. Just as paired dancers must move in time and tempo with each other to create a beautiful scene, so must managers and team members move in time with each other. Paired dancers trust that the other will be there, will be where he/she is supposed to be and will not be in the wrong place, stepping on feet or worse. In the world of work and service providing, timing and placement are just as critical. Deliverables may not be a dance performance, but they are performed.

REFLECTION POINT:
Managing Talent

✓ What is your management credo?

_____

_____

_____

✓ How do you put that into action?

_____

_____

_____

✓ What response do you get from your staff?

_____

_____

_____

✓ Consider the best, most effective staff member you have. How do you engage with him/her?

_____

_____

_____

✓ Consider the most trying staff member you have, the one who is struggling. How do you engage with him/her?

_____

_____

_____

✓ If they are the same, what room do you have to adjust your practices with the struggling staff member?

_____

_____

_____

✓ If they are different, what can you learn from your practices with successful staff that you can apply to your struggling staff member?

_____

_____

_____

By the way, not everyone is a born manager. There is no shame in that. Management and leadership can be learned. It is much more productive to identify someone in a management position who isn't prepared for it and offer them advanced training and support than to leave them there, under-performing. There is also no shame in identifying someone as not a manager. Not everyone is cut out for it. There is nothing wrong with that. Position your people for success, whether that is as a people manager or not. Find their strength, their super power, and lead with that!

- 49% of HR leaders named retention and leadership development programs as the top priority among talent management goals (Saba Software)
- 78% of employees feel they are making a difference and appreciated when managers focus on their strengths over their weaknesses (The VIA Institute on Character)
- 64% of employees believe they will be more successful at work by building on their strengths than fixing their weaknesses (The VIA Institute on Character)
- 65% of employees who report having had a meaningful discussion with their manager about their strengths describe themselves as flourishing at work (The VIA Institute on Character)

Career Path/ Professional Growth

The world is your oyster. Many of us have been told that since childhood. We work hard in school, we search for the right job, we are ready to give it our all. Then what happens? With luck, we are hired by someone who sees the value we bring and encourages our growth. With luck, we are heard, and our vision is realized as others offer us a hand, a word of encouragement, an opportunity for us to grow and shine. This is also what happens, not with luck, but with an engaged employer. Engaged employers invest in their people and challenge them to reach new heights.

I heard an executive speak a few months back. He was challenging his team to increase their hiring by 25%. The leaders in the room were sullen. "We aren't seeing the type of candidates we need," they reported.

Aside from addressing the recruiting methods, this executive looked straight at the team and asked. "Show of hands. How many of you are doing what you went to college to do?" Not one hand raised. "Wait a minute. You are telling me that your education didn't fully prepare you for the job you have today? No, of course it didn't. You need to recruit talent. You need to find people who have the skills and the desire to do the work we are doing. Then, you must train them!"

He was right on. What this executive was telling his team is that you recruit for skill and will, and then you refine the skill and the will grows. Bring in talented people with enough ability to perform and who can learn advanced and adjacent skills. By offering them the opportunity and giving them the training to advance, you are investing in your business, your employees, and ultimately the service you provide to your customers. You are also building your relationship and creating loyalty within your team.

- 32% of employers have seen an increase in retention as a result of increasing their educational requirements (CareerBuilder)
- 25% of employers have seen an increase in customer loyalty as a result of increasing employee educational requirements (CareerBuilder)
- 68% of employers offer training programs; 71% offer soft skills and 72% offer hard skills (CareerBuilder)
- Employees who get the opportunity to continually develop are twice as likely to say they will spend their career with their company (Gallup)
- Of the 35% of employers who trained low-skill workers and hired them for high-skill jobs in 2015, 33% plan to do the same this year (CareerBuilder)
- 40% of employers are sending employees back to school to get an advanced degree (23% fund it partially, 12% fully funding) (CareerBuilder)
- 53% of millennials say learning new things or having access to professional development opportunities would make them stay at their job (EdAssist)

So what about a career path? Sure skill development leads to advanced work opportunities, but does that equate to a career path? Sometimes yes, sometimes no. A career path is just what it sounds like–a clear path to career development. This is when roles are not static, but grow and change over time. Promotion is one of the keys to career path, but it is not the only one. Successful, engaged employees see their path to growth. A career path includes advanced training, enhanced responsibility, additional recognition, and yes, eventually an increase in pay and title. Nobody wants to be doing the exact same job day in and day out for the next five years. There is no intellectual or intrinsic reward to that.

- 60% of HR leaders believe that their companies provide employees with a clear career path; just 36% of employees agree (Saba Software)
- 93% of US adults say they left their employer in order to change roles (Gallup)
- 12% of employees feel their employers aid them in their career development (Bridge)

REFLECTION POINT:

Growing Talent

✓ What do the career paths look like in your organization?

_____

_____

✓ How can your team members see where and how they can be contributing in new and creative ways in the future?

_____

_____

_____

✓ What training plans or methods to identify skill-building opportunities for your team members are in place? When is the last time they were updated?

_____

_____

_____

✓ How do you define upward mobility?

_____

_____

_____

✓ When was the last time you promoted a team member?

_____

_____

_____

✓ When was the last time you celebrated the team's or a team member's success?

_____

_____

_____

What do you feel called to do now? What actions could you take today to demonstrate your commitment to talent growth in your organization?

Workplace Environment

The basis of the workplace environment comes from the operationalization of your organizational values. We dug into those earlier in the book. I offered you the analogy of a garden. You are the gardener, and it is your responsibility to tend to the field in order to bear fruit and bountiful crops. If you are delivering a service, and you have made the commitment to educate and promote your team members, you are well on your way. Now, let's take a look at the actual environment your team is working in. Is it optimally configured for success?

REFLECTION POINT:

Environment Scan

✓ What does your organizational structure look like?

_____

_____

_____

✓ Does it mirror the workflow and the communication?

_____

_____

_____

✓ What work processes are in place? Do they flow easily or are there choke-points?

_____

_____

_____

✓ What technology do you use to support your work processes? Do they help or hinder?

_____

_____

_____

✓ What is your meeting cadence? Are you spending time hearing new information, creating new solutions, or just reviewing old statuses?

_____

_____

_____

✓ Where is work done? Is everyone working in a comfortable place? Is collaboration supported? Is individual work time respected? What boundaries are in place?

_____

_____

_____

Every work environment is different. The optimal work environment for your team will look like no other. Sure you may have qualities that exist in other organizations, but no other organization is your organization. Following a map that another used will get you nowhere. You are not starting at the same place and your end goal is not the same. This is where you must customize your plan so that it works for you and your team.

What will make your team love not only what they do, but how they do it? What will make your team fall in love with work every single day?

"The only way to do great work is to love what you do."
STEVE JOBS

P.S. If this sounds challenging, and if you have any lingering doubts about the bottom line impact of investing, I offer you the following research finding: Employee engagement programs can increase profits by $2400 per employee per year (Workplace Research Foundation)

CHAPTER 7:

Becoming a Collaborative Alpha: Allowing the Team to Lead

"Often the best solution to a management problem is the right person."
EDWIN BOOZ

ello again, CEO. I'm glad you are still with me. We have covered the ground needed for your organization to flourish. Now it is time to talk about you. Now it is time to settle in, admire what you have built, love yourself for all you have been and done, take a deep breath and let it go. Because now you are on the part of the journey where you get to grow. Your personal transformation is continuing and you are now at the metamorphosis from caterpillar to butterfly. It is time for you to let go of what *is,* in order to be open to what's *next.* You will only grab the brass ring if you are able and willing to let go of the reins. I hope you are ready!

This opportunity for self-innovation and re-birth is exciting! Ok, it may be a little scary, but not for you. You have already taken the biggest leaps out there. This is a leap inward. This is the investment you make in yourself. I told you that your team members were your first customers, and that is true. But what comes before your first customer? You. The service provider. If you are not healthy, happy, and whole, you can't provide service. You can't function.

Secure Your Position Of Strength

Leading can only happen from a position of strength. You are familiar with this position as you've spent significant time there. As you know, it is not possible to lead from a position of fear. Fear closes you down, thwarts creativity, and limits choices to those of survival. The same is true for shame, anger, self-doubt, and worry (all brothers and sisters to fear). Fear is the real "F-word." I think you know this and you are no stranger to looking fear in the face and walking right by it. After all, you zoomed past dozens of fears to get where you are today. Only today, as the leader of other souls, you have new responsibilities and with them, new fears emerge. So it is only right to pause and listen quietly to see if there are any new fears knocking on your door.

Once again in your journey, it is time to identify, name, acknowledge and then release your fears. This will make room for courage to accompany you in the driver's seat. What makes this a little tricky to execute is that fear is sly; it often masquerades itself as security, logic, patience, a plan B. It encourages you to hedge. It provides tons of evidence why hedging is the right thing to do, the smart thing to do, the safe thing to do, maybe even the kind thing to do in regard to people management. However, to hedge your bets as a leader is actually hedging your bet on yourself and your team. There is nothing smart, safe or kind about that.

When fear causes you to delay action, it is pushing you into false steps. You may recognize them as false steps because they are slow and not easy to take. Those steps do not indicate leading from a position of strength, rather being stuck in the fear zone.

A leader looks fear in the eye and says, *thanks for the warning, I appreciate you looking out for me and heightening my senses. Yes, you're right, the only thing scarier than losing is winning – because then I have to do this job, and then I have to show the world who I really am. Then, I can hide no more. Thanks for the reminder that I get to be real, and I get to choose who and how I am every day. Thanks, Fear, but today I'm leaving you on the shelf and putting Courage on instead.*

A position of strength means having no fear about clearly stating the needs (of oneself, of the business, of the client) and meeting them. That's the beauty of being the leader – you have the ability to make choices about your operating environment, the culture you are nurturing, and the team members you select. You can choose to surround yourself with people who will outshine you in different aspects, and you can choose to rely upon all of their gifts to contribute to the organization you create. You can choose to amplify all that you are with all that they are. There is nothing to fear about smart, talented people; they are the people you are working hard to recruit and retain. When you respect their gifts, and celebrate them, you will keep them close.

Grant Yourself Permission

You are in control of your position. You give yourself permission to be in control, which also means you give yourself permission to *let go*. You give yourself permission to know what you know, to not know everything, and to live in questions that empower you to learn, explore, love and lead. What's magical about this, is that you also give yourself permission to not *like* everything and not be happy *all* the time. You give yourself permission to be honest and authentic and to tell it like it is (to yourself and to others). Resilience is not about always being happy or putting on the rose-colored glasses. Resilience is the ability to admit when things are less than optimal and then choose how to be in them.

When the chips are down, what kind of leader do you want to be? Who do you want to be for your team? This doesn't translate to stay the course and be static where you are. It means acknowledge the truth, so you can get a different perspective. If it is not "all good", admit it. Then you are free to explore other options that could bring improvement. By all means, do not keep calm and carry on, unless you are in love with the status quo.

Keeping calm and carrying on is the false perception that everything will be back to normal soon. The fact is, nothing goes back, only forward, and "normal" is ever-changing. Nothing remains the same – we are living and leading in a constantly changing world. To carry on as you did last year is to be outdated–it is the recipe for failure. You are using last year's solution for this year's problems. Check your sensors. You are in control, and you have the ability to say, *No, sorry, this time I'm calm, and cool, but this time, carrying on won't suffice. This time, I'm making a change. I'm shaking it up.*

Engage the Power of Forgiveness

Forgiveness is a powerful thing. It doesn't change what has happened; it changes what is to come. The act of forgiveness lifts the darkness from our souls, so that they are free to dance again.

When things go wrong, we often replay the scenario again and again in our minds. *Why did he do X? Why did she say that? Didn't they know that would hurt me? Why did this happen?* There are no real answers to these questions. And if you find some, they won't bring you peace. There is really only one thing that can allow you to turn the page and move on, and that is to forgive. When you forgive, you release the thoughts, the emotions, and the sensations of anger or dread. You set free all the energy, the brain power, and the cells that were working so hard to seek an answer. You release all the energy that was tied up in generating the feelings of hurt, anger, distrust, and skepticism. You stop hurting yourself over something you didn't do. That's the amazing thing about forgiveness. It grants grace and peace to both the victim and the perpetrator. Both are set free in one act of love.

You can't forgive without loving. And I don't mean sentimentality. I don't mean mush. I mean having enough courage to stand up and say, 'I forgive. I'm finished with it.'
-MAYA ANGELOU

When we think of forgiveness, we often thing of forgiving someone who has wronged us: a friend, an ex-lover, a sibling, or a former colleague. We think of someone who has been allowed into our inner sanctum and trusted with our precious selves, and who didn't protect us or honor the relationship as we had expected. This act of forgiveness allows us to remain open to the world and to trust again. It is allows to not have our hearts grow hard so people slide off of us.

There is another type of forgiveness that is equally, and possibly even more important. This is self-forgiveness. We are not taught self-forgiveness, nor are we practiced in it. We instead perseverate on what went wrong, and question ourselves, asking "Why?" Why did I make that mistake? Why didn't I know? What if I had done this? If only I knew that! How did I let that happen? If it wasn't bad enough that something went wrong, we have programmed ourselves to repeatedly think about these things and feel badly over and over again. To what end?

Self-forgiveness is a learned skill. It requires loving yourself, which also may require some practice. It is easier to forgive another than to forgive yourself. Often we hold ourselves to a higher standard – expecting more from ourselves than others. So, to give yourself grace and peace and offer yourself forgiveness is possibly the greatest act of self-love. Allowing yourself to forgive yourself also provides you access to feel the power of your own love.

REFLECTION POINT:
Self Forgiveness

Take a moment to reflect on what may have not gone as you would have hoped. With the knowledge and understanding that you did the best you could with the information you had at the time, receive the gift that time and perspective have granted you.

Start small and practice.

✓ I forgive myself for…

_____

_____

_____

✓ I am grateful for what I learned…

_____

_____

_____

✓ Now I know…

_____

_____

_____

✓ I am empowered to be…

_____

_____

_____

Release yourself from the suffering that comes from the pain of carrying guilt. It is impossible to *grow* from that place. It is impossible to *lead* from that place. It is impossible to *love* from that place. As you practice forgiving yourself, you will grow in strength, and what once seemed impossible will be quite possible.

When I am confronted with a memory of something I wish I had done differently or chosen differently, I remind myself of a personal mantra: *"I did the best I could with what I knew and had available to me at the time. My intention was good. For all that went wrong, I forgive myself."* I have learned recently that it is very powerful to then clarify what I learned from the situation and to be grateful for that. *"I learned so much from (X experience), and built my strength in (fill in the blank)... for that I am grateful."*

As leaders, this exercise of self-forgiveness can be repeated whenever necessary, until it is no longer necessary.

The weak can never forgive. Forgiveness is the attribute of the strong.
-MAHATMA GANDHI

Discover the Beauty of Boundaries

In the workplace, boundaries are made and broken time and again. Somehow we got the idea that boundaries are the equivalent of "command and control," or hierarchy. They aren't. The most generous, available leaders are also the ones with the firmest boundaries. They hold the line. They know the power of accountability. They will show up on time, every time, for their people, and they expect the same in return.

Many of us have a wrong idea in our heads. We believe that if we don't sacrifice our boundaries to help others, we will be acting in an unkind way and will be unloved, disliked, and not respected. The fact is, the opposite is true. Boundaries are what ensure your ability to show up with integrity and generosity every time. Brené Brown has conducted excellent research on this, and I commend her work to you for reading. The leaders who establish and hold their boundaries are the most well-loved, respected, and sought-after leaders there are. They are consistent in their thoughts, words and deeds, and they model a way of being in the business that communicates ease and grace. They lead by example.

One final scenario provides a concise illustration of the power of boundaries. Mike leads a large business. He has several direct reports and dozens of team members. If Mike wanted to, he could be answering emails and reviewing documents 16 hours a day. Guess what? Mike used to do that. Without boundaries in place, Mike's work tasks bled into nearly every waking hour of his day. It was so easy to do with his smartphone on hand at all times. It led to a decline in his health, stress in his family, and surprisingly the loss of a client. Mike realized that these practices did not serve anyone well. By being "on" all the time, he never had time to re-energize. He also made unreasonable demands of his team. His family was not happy about the absent/tired/cranky/distracted husband/father they had either. Mike decided to make some changes. Because he relied heavily on his calendar, that was the natural construct for him to use to systematically make and communicate change. Mike established working hours, consultation hours, family time, free time, and sleep time. They are not all the same, and they don't overlap! Once Mike established these, shared them, and held to them, everything changed. Because he began every day with some quiet time, he had clear goals and objectives for his day. He was no longer negotiating minutes, but moving through his day with purpose and ease. He was able to answer questions with a yes or a no, equally comfortable with both answers, because all of his decisions were in alignment with his purpose. His work became more efficient, his team felt like they got a new boss, his family felt joy again, and Mike's physical health and emotional well-being had marked improvements. I should also mention that his business portfolio doubled. That may seem counter-intuitive, but that is how it works. Clients liked this purposeful, even-keeled leader. Mike set clear intentions for himself and his business, and his boundaries were both a reflection of and a reinforcement to his intention. He had exactly the right amount of time for everything that mattered and nothing that didn't.

REFLECTION POINT:
Healthy Boundaries

✓ What boundaries do you currently have in place?

_____

_____

_____

✓ How are they serving you? your team? your clients?

_____

_____

_____

✓ How are they reflected in your business processes?

_____

_____

_____

✓ If you have compromised your boundaries, what brought you to that decision?

_____

_____

_____

✓ What did that feel like?

_____

_____

_____

✓ What was the result?

_____

_____

_____

✓ If faced with this situation again, what could be done within your boundaries?

_____

_____

_____

✓ What boundaries might you want to revisit?

_____

_____

_____

Once these boundaries are established and maintained, you can then effectively add and execute other critical tasks such as innovating new business processes and service offerings, and stepping away in trust that your team will stand and deliver, whether you are there or not.

The question is, are you ready? My answer: Yes, you are. I know this because you are here.

Go ahead, CEO, let go. Let the plans you have so carefully made take flight. Let the garden you have planted and tended bloom. Allow yourself to move from the caterpillar exploring the soil and ensuring the ground is solid and transition to the butterfly. Fly now, about your garden and admire its beauty. Enjoy the 30,000-foot view, and begin to envision what is next.

MY WISH FOR YOU

You already know that you have my complete admiration. You've breathed life into your own vision and dream and invited others to share in that with you. You are the embodiment of service. For this alone, I am grateful for you and your contribution to society.

I hope that the same fierce energy and courage you summoned to build your business and step into your role as leader will now be used to invest in your people, time and again. The more you show up for them, the more they will show up for you, and the customers you set out to serve will receive tenfold what you could deliver on your own. In developing your people you are multiplying the impact of your leadership and your gifts in the world, and you are offering a platform for their best to shine.

This choice will bring you great joy. My wish for you is that you choose joy and open yourself to this part of the journey.

ACKNOWLEDGEMENTS

"Working hard for something we don't care about is called stress; working hard for something we love is called passion."
-SIMON SINEK

Sometimes all it takes is someone to ask you a good question for magic to happen in your life. I am grateful for all of the good questions I have been asked this year, and the inspiration they provided for this book to be born.

I am blessed beyond measure, and truly grateful for my family– the one I was born into, the one I built, and the ones I have joined. Everything happens through love; and one thing I have no shortage of is love.

A special thank you goes out to my many coaches and colleagues who have provided that perfect balance of challenge and support– encouraging me to bring my best self to the world each and every day. One special coach challenged me to be my future self every single day, and to enact all that I teach relentlessly. I took that to heart, because she saw in me what I couldn't see for myself. Ah, the value of coaches.

To one of my oldest and dearest friends, who saved me from myself during high school calculus, once again, saved me from myself and my errant commas and love of run-on sentences. Thank you, Colleen.

To the Morgan James publishing team, David Hancock, CEO & Founder, and Megan Malone, Managing Editor, thank you for the support and guidance through the publishing process.

To the Difference Press team, especially Angela Lauria, Kate Makled, and Maggie McReynolds, I appreciate your love and support throughout the process of becoming an author.

Words of love that can never be sufficient go to my first teachers and advocates: my parents, to the spitfire who brightens my every day–my daughter Angelina Jane, and to my partner in life, Steve.

To you, dear reader, I am grateful. Thank you for spending this time with me.

ABOUT THE AUTHOR

Janeen M. Latini, best-selling author of *Love to Lead. Lead to Love.*, is a certified leadership coach who specializes in working with leaders, teams, and organizations during times of change. She prepares leaders to be successful in high-visibility, high-pressure situations, while finding balance in their everyday lives. Her clients appreciate her candor and her commitment to supporting them in bringing their best selves forward in work and in life.

A certified Leadership Coach, change management practitioner, management consultant, and published author and playwright, she brings 20 years of applied experience and a whole-hearted approach to her practice. In harmony with her work as a leadership coach, her consulting practice includes change management, strategic communications, organizational development, process improvement, adult learning, and group facilitation. Janeen is a seasoned project manager and has lead teams over 100 people delivering cross-functional services to clients. She is a skilled account manager, having successfully built and managed business portfolios of $30M/year. She has worked with public, private, not-for-profit, and commercial clients.

Janeen previously served as the Program Manager for Booz Allen Hamilton's Center for Change Management, where she led investments in intellectual capital, staff development, and industry relations. She holds a BA in Psychology, and an MA in Organizational Development from The George Washington University; is an Associate Certified Coach by the International Coach Federation; a Certified Leadership Coach and a Certified Change Management Advanced Practitioner by Georgetown University. Janeen is a founding member of the Association of Change Management Professionals (ACMP), and was a speaker at the 2013 ACMP Global Conference: *Coaching Leaders Through Change*. Janeen served as Co-Chair of Georgetown University's Institute for Transformational Leadership 2014 Graduate Coaches Conference: *Resilience: Coaching Leaders Through Challenging Times*.

Janeen's coaching approach focuses on overall wellness, and operates from the belief that each person can achieve whatever he/she dreams. At the heart of this practice is the belief that imagination is far more powerful than willpower and to truly reach one's potential, authentic, creative energy must be tapped and used.

Janeen's first book, **Love to Lead. Lead to Love.** presents her Five Totems of Leadership as guiding principles to support leaders on their journey. Janeen often uses these totems and related practices to enrich coaching engagements. In this, her second book, **Stack It Up!** she applies her leadership principals to arguably the most expensive challenge in business today: retaining top talent. She actively coaches leaders faced with this challenge and supports them in building and sustaining profitable businesses and teams.

Janeen is dedicated to helping leaders find and experience joy in their lives. She designed a program "From Stuck to Skyrocket" for those who have experienced a lull in their career path and who want to re-energize their path. She is also passionate about supporting women leaders, especially working moms and has developed "You Got This", a program to support them.

A lover of coffee, gardens, the Jersey Shore at sunset, and midnight conversations, Janeen lives in gratitude. A student of meditation, a creative chef, and a proud mom, she lives in Arlington, VA with her beloved daughter and their rescue kitties, rescue puppies, and fish.

THANK YOU

An Invitation:

If you share this passion for retaining top talent and growing your business, let's be in touch. Visit me at www.latinileadership.com.

To access my free audio class on retention, visit: www.latinileadership.com/stackitupoffer

At the end of this session you will be able to:

- Articulate your goals for retention
- Evaluate potential actions to support those goals
- Determine your next steps

Morgan James
Speakers Group

www.TheMorganJamesSpeakersGroup.com

We connect Morgan James published
authors with live and online events
and audiences who will benefit
from their expertise.

Printed in the USA
CPSIA information can be obtained
at www.ICGtesting.com
JSHW082357140824
68134JS00020B/2133